DINNER WITH CECILE AND WILLIAM

THE TRAVELING GOURMAND SERIES

1. *The Gluten-Free Way: My Way,* by William Maltese & Adrienne Z. Milligan
2. *Back of the Boat Gourmet Cooking: Afloat—Pool-Side—Backyard,* by Bonnie Clark & William Maltese
3. *William Maltese's Wine Taster's Diary: Spokane/Pullman Washington Wine Region,* by William Maltese
4. *In Search of the Perfect Pinot G! Australia's Mornington Peninsula: William Maltese's Wine Taster's Guide #2,* by A. B. Gayle & William Maltese
5. *Whole Wheat for Food Storage: Recipes for Unground Wheat,* by Michael R. Collings & Judith Collings
6. *Even Gourmands Have to Diet: It's Just Food, People!,* by Bonnie Clark and William Maltese
7. *Dinner with Cecile and William: A Cookbook,* by Cecile Charles and William Maltese

DINNER WITH CECILE AND WILLIAM

A COOKBOOK

CECILE CHARLES & WILLIAM MALTESE

THE BORGO PRESS
MMXII

DINNER WITH CECILE AND WILLIAM

Copyright © 2012 by Cecile Charles and William Maltese
Cover art by Cecile Charles

FIRST EDITION

Published by Wildside Press LLC

www.wildsidebooks.com

DEDICATION

For foodies everywhere,
and YOU know who you are.

And for Cynthia, Cecile's sister, just because.

CONTENTS

INTRODUCTION: William Maltese 9
INTRODUCTION: Cecile Charles 11
SEASONINGS 15
GARNISHES 27
HORS D'ŒUVRES 49
PÂTÉS 61
BREADS-ROLLS-CREPES-CHIPS-PIE CRUSTS-
    THICKENERS-DOUGH 77
NATURAL DRINKS 105
MAIN COURSES 115
CASSEROLES 131
STEWS 149
SOUPS 169
SALADS 185
SIDE DISHES 199
DESSERTS 209
RECIPE INDEX 227

AUTHORS' BIOS 233

INTRODUCTION
WILLIAM MALTESE

Anyone who enjoys gourmet cooking, and who always yearns to experience an adventure when/while eating it, like I do, is exceedingly lucky whenever he finds a kindred spirit, professional or otherwise, who can spice things up with good and unique food, coupled with good wine and good conversation. Otherwise, faced constantly with boors, disinterested in adventurous eating, in eating well, unappreciative of fine wine, and incapable of scintillating conversation, one might just as well stay at home, prepare and eat his or her own food, drink his or her own wine, and talk to him- or herself.

There are many professional chefs who spend their lives on television, and/or in professional kitchens, wowing the public with their cooking artistry. There are those who aren't professionals but who still cook and, actually, invent their own recipes, and who mainly slip public notice, because they and their food aren't on display 24/7. This book introduces you to Cecile Charles, once one of the former, now one of the latter: a gourmet-cook extraordinaire who has invented, and still invents, her own recipes and whose culinary creativity always leaves me inspired and astounded whenever she joins me in the kitchen or at the dining table.

INTRODUCTION
CECILE CHARLES

So, hello, readers.

I'm Cecile Charles, lover of good gourmet food that surprises by a use of unusual mixtures of ingredients.

As a younger person, I spent time in several fine establishments, learning to cook food in unexpected ways. Taught to explore flavors and how they blend with each other, I spent copious amounts of time mixing ingredients, to see how the results tasted. Initially, I, more often than not, ended up with horrible-tasting food, but once I got the hang of blending, I more and more often struck culinary gold.

When one works, professionally, as a cook in a good restaurant, or hotel, as I once did, one is inevitably expected to enter food contests. This I did. Through such blue-ribbon winning experiences, I confirmed that I was adept at doing what I do. Combined with an artist's eye (my other eye "analytical"), I made, and still do, unusual foods that not only taste good, and are good for you, but look beautiful as well.

When I worked as a chef, my unusual menu items kept the customers coming back for more, kept me secure in my job, and saw my list of innovative recipes grow. Yet, it was difficult for me, having learned cooking on-the-job, to compete with the newer chefs coming out of college with their official academic training, certified diplomas, and willingness to work for less pay; so, I began hoarding my unique recipes, thinking I would eventually open my own business.

While I was cooking professionally, I was, also, professionally painting (this book's cover one of my works). Of those two chief passions, painting began to take precedence, until I found myself painting every day, cooking less often and less inventively, and eventually making the decision to embrace art, not food, full time.

I married and for years devoted myself primarily to being a housewife, and, while not giving up painting and cooking, doing both of those for pleasure instead of for money.

At this time of my life, I own and run, with the assistance of my dedicated team, *The Heart of Spokane,* an arts and antiques boutique, that sells my artworks and the artwork of others (http://www.theheartofspokane.com), as well as all kinds of up-cycled "green' things, and everything vintage. Also, I write, dance, sing, am funny (so they say, but who are "they" anyway?), and play musical instruments whenever I can squeeze in some extra time (or, with my return to inventive cooking, do I mean thyme?).

If, over the years, I have resurrected one of my original recipes, or two, for some special event or the other, I seldom, ever, considered giving away any of my secret "babies", or even writing them down in cookbook format, figuring them safest locked away, from prying eyes, in my head.

Then I met William Maltese, one of those natural gourmands fortunate enough to have travelled a good deal in the world, during the course of his prolific career as a writer that includes authoring a series of cookbooks and a *WILLIAM MALTESE WINE TASTER'S DIARY* series for the Wildside/Borgo Press's "The Traveling Gourmand" imprint, in which this book is included. Meeting him, a man who has tasted unique foods from so many different countries, saw me suddenly eager to see what I could do to pique his admittedly experienced (and jaded?) palate; I wanted to know if he could be as wowed as others less "into" food had been. So, I planned a fun evening of surprise tastings for him and Bonnie Clark, his co-author of *BACK OF THE BOAT GOURMET COOKING.*

I served him mushrooms stuffed with Cucumber Pâté, Simple Butter Croissants, Mushroom Apple Soup, Weed Salad, Bleuet Persil Soup, Red Radish Roast Chunk Vegetable Aperitif, Tomato Shrimp Aspic, Chicken Cordon Bleu Casserole, and Golden Rhum Vanille Pudding. I received the best compliment when, in an offhanded way (for that's William's nature), he said, "Well, do we have, here, I wonder, another of my cookbooks in the making?" I assumed it was purely complimentary, not an actual invitation to publish with him, but, once I had slept on it, I actually had the epiphany that decided it might be time for me to break down my previous fetish for secrecy and actually share with William, and, more importantly, with others.

And, as it turned out, William, as luck would have it, was more than serious about my joining him in a cookbook, spotlighting my years of innovative cooking, this book the result.

For those of you who cook a great deal, you know good food does good things for your body. If you want great energy, you need energy-producing foods. If you want, literally, to sweat out the toxins inside of you, that requires yet another type of food. Many of this book's recipes are good for digestion, and for bringing a balance of nutrients to your system. If you want an increased libido, we recommend dishes for that, too...all in this cookbook. We specifically point out many of these benefits as we go along.

I'm not going to be silly enough to insist that William and I have come up with a food to cure each and every ailment, but we do believe food can, our food can, provide the right answers to all kinds of health questions.

Our recipes are full of fresh, not canned, foods, are best served as three-ounce servings, per http://www.choosemyplate.gov, and need be mixed and matched with other food groups for well-rounded meals. While we've sorted through many recipes, to come up with those we've picked for inclusion, here, we've decided to include, just for the hell of it, some of the funniest-sounding dishes, some of William and my favorites, and some we've just thrown in—a couple of my Granny's recipes—for good measure (Granny having been a great influence in my cooking). Last, but not least, we've included a couple of suggestions you might be reluctant to try, but which we dare you to give a chance.

That said.... Here's to the enjoyment of inventive gourmet cooking...good eating...sublime drinking...and the enjoyment of good conversation and bonhomie with equally adventuresome friends and family.

SEASONINGS

Good foodies prep their seasoning closet with spices and seasonings in advance of cooking certain recipes.

Having a nice grouping of different flavorings on hand reduces the need to do guess work, later, when a specific flavor is needed. Besides a filled-to-the-brim cabinet of usable spices impresses the heck out of people who stop by for dinner. Sometimes, when we're feeling particularly mischievous, we ask a guest to please fetch us the salt and pepper shakers, just so they can take a look at our impressive spice cabinets.

Don't forget, "basic drying" means a warm dry place and a cover of cheesecloth as a way for air to circulate around the ingredients. A poor man's drying screen consists of two wire sieves stacked one inside the other.

Here are some easy shortcuts for getting your cupboard adequately stocked with necessary seasoning required for the recipes in our book.

Arabian Spice

Ingredients:

⅓ cup white pepper (freshly ground is best)
⅓ cup ground coriander
¼ cup ground cinnamon
¼ cup ground cloves
½ cup ground cumin
3 Tablespoons ground cardamom
¼ cup ground nutmeg
½ cup paprika (or part cayenne, depending on taste)
¼ cup turmeric
1 Tablespoon ground ginger
1 Tablespoon allspice
1 Tablespoon broken bay leaf, ground
1 Tablespoon dried and ground dates
¼ cup dried limes, peel remove seeds, grind

Directions:

Combine ingredients.

Roast in a dry sauté pan.

Cool.

Store in tightly lidded jar.

Cajun Spice

Ingredients:

1 teaspoon fennel seeds, ground
1 teaspoon cumin seeds, ground

1 teaspoon mustard seeds, ground
2 teaspoons NapaStyle® gray sea salt
2 teaspoons dried and ground garlic clove
2½ teaspoons paprika
1 teaspoon ground black pepper
1 teaspoon dried and ground onion
1 teaspoon cayenne pepper
1¼ teaspoons dried oregano
1¼ teaspoons dried thyme
½ teaspoon red pepper (medium hot)
½ teaspoon ginger
½ teaspoon ground clove
¼ teaspoon ground sage

Directions:

Combine ingredients.

Mix.

Store in tightly lidded jar.

Curry Spice

Ingredients:

4 Tablespoons coriander seeds
2 Tablespoons cumin seeds
2 Tablespoons black peppercorns
2 teaspoons mustard seeds
2 dried hot chili peppers
1 teaspoon ground ginger
1 teaspoon ground turmeric

Directions:

Combine the whole seeds in a dry skillet and roast over moderate heat until lightly browned.

Cool.

Grind roasted seeds with remaining chili peppers.

Add remaining ingredients.

Keep refrigerated in a tightly lidded jar.

English Spice

Although this spice blend is mostly used for baking, we also use it with pork or chicken.

Ingredients:

½ teaspoon cinnamon
1 Tablespoon allspice
1 Tablespoon coriander seeds
2 teaspoons ground cloves
2 teaspoon ground mace
2 teaspoon freshly grated nutmeg
2 teaspoon ground ginger

Directions:

Combine ingredients.

Mix.

Store in tightly lidded jar.

Hawaiian Spice

Ingredients:

2 Tablespoons fennel seeds
2 Tablespoons cloves
2 Tablespoons cinnamon
2 Tablespoons white pepper
2 Tablespoons ginger
4 Tablespoons dried pineapple, ground
2 teaspoons dried parsley, ground
2 teaspoons dried onion, ground
2 teaspoons allspice

Directions:

Combine all ingredients.

Mix.

Store in tightly lidded jar.

Indian Spice (India)

This is a catch-all spice mix, good for most savory dishes.

Ingredients:

1 Tablespoon salt
1 Tablespoon ground ginger
1 Tablespoon ground saffron
1 Tablespoon ground onion
1 Tablespoon ground garlic
1 Tablespoon ground nutmeg

1 Tablespoon ground cloves
1 Tablespoon ground cilantro
1 Tablespoon ground black pepper
1 Tablespoon ground cumin
1 Tablespoon ground mustard Seed
1 Tablespoon ground asafetida (hing)
1 Tablespoon ground cayenne
1 Tablespoon ground star anise
1 Tablespoon ground fenugreek seeds
1 Tablespoon ground coriander
1 Tablespoon ground chilies

Directions

Combine ingredients.

Mix.

Store in tightly lidded jar.

Italian Spice

Ingredients:

3 Tablespoons dried basil
3 Tablespoons dried oregano
3 Tablespoons dried parsley
1 Tablespoon garlic powder
1 teaspoon onion powder
1 teaspoon dried thyme
1 teaspoon dried rosemary
¼ teaspoon black pepper
¼ teaspoon red-pepper flakes

Directions:

Combine ingredients.

Mix.

Store in a tightly lidded jar.

Korean Spice

Instructions:

5 Tablespoons untoasted sesame seeds.
6 scallions (spring onions), dried
1 teaspoon rice vinegar
1 Tablespoon sugar
1 teaspoon NapaStyle® gray sea salt
1 garlic clove, crushed and dried
1 dried hot pepper, ground

Directions:

Toast sesame seeds. Preferably don't buy them pre-toasted at the store; the taste difference between the one and the other is genuinely noticeable.

Cool.

Soak dried scallions and sesame seeds in the rice vinegar. Let dry.

Cut roots off scallions and refrigerate for anther recipe.

Grind dried scallion leaves.

Add ground scallion leaves to sugar, NapaStyle gray sea salt, garlic, and hot pepper.

Store in a tightly lidded jar.

Mediterranean Spice

Ingredients:

3 Tablespoons dried rosemary
2 Tablespoons ground cumin
2 Tablespoons ground coriander
1 Tablespoon dried oregano
2 teaspoons ground cinnamon
½ teaspoon NapaStyle® gray sea salt

Directions:

Combine all ingredients in a bowl.

Mix.

Store in tightly lidded jar.

Mexican Spice

Ingredients:

½ cup chili powder
¼ cup sweet paprika
1 Tablespoon ground cumin
1½ teaspoons garlic powder
1 teaspoon onion powder
1 teaspoon ground dried chipotle chili pepper
2 teaspoons dried oregano leaves, ground

1 teaspoon NapaStyle® gray sea salt

Directions:

Combine ingredients.

Mix.

Store in tightly lidded jar.

Oriental Spice

Ingredients:

2 teaspoons Sichuan peppers
3 star anise
2 teaspoon fennel seeds
5 cloves, ground
1 teaspoon fresh ground cinnamon
1 teaspoon NapaStyle® gray sea salt
½ teaspoon white pepper

Directions

Combine ingredients.

Roast.

Cool.

Store in a tightly lidded jar.

Red-Pepper Flakes

These are hot, and so much better when hand-made.

Do not make the mistake of rubbing your eyes while crushing these peppers; the burn doesn't go away without soaking your face in water for several hours.

Ingredients:

1 pound Cayenne peppers

Directions:

Crush peppers.

Finally chop crushed peppers (do not remove the seeds).

Put between two cooking screens and leave in a warm place.

Dry for several days.

Store in a tightly lidded jar.

Savory Salt

Ingredients:

1 Tablespoon black pepper
1 Tablespoon celery seeds, ground
1 Tablespoon onion salt
1½ teaspoons garlic salt
1½ teaspoons orange peel, ground
1½ teaspoons sugar
1 teaspoon NapaStyle® gray sea salt

½ teaspoon white pepper
½ teaspoon dill weed
½ teaspoon dried thyme, ground
¼ teaspoon dried lemon zest, ground
¼ teaspoon cayenne pepper
½ teaspoon celery salt

Directions:

Combine ingredients.

Mix.

Store in tightly lidded jar.

Vegetable Spice

Ingredients:

1½ teaspoon dried onion, ground
1½ teaspoon toasted sesame seeds, ground
1 teaspoon chives, dried, ground
1 teaspoon tarragon, dried, ground
1½ teaspoon mustard seed, ground
1½ teaspoon dill weed, dried and ground
1½ teaspoon dried red-pepper flakes, ground
1 teaspoon oregano, ground

Directions

Combine ingredients.

Mix.

Store in a tightly lidded jar.

GARNISHES

Garnishes are those yummy little dollops of extra gooeyness that we all view as "must-haves" on our foods. In America, since the advent of artificial dollops, they are often full of calories, but our garnish recipes are a blends of ingredients intended to accent flavor

NOTE: A "dollop" is no more than one Tablespoon; think petit in size but grand in flavor.

Almond Crème

This is a pretty speckled red and green and is a wonderful garnish during holidays. Also, it's a nice finish on crème soups.

Ingredients:

10 Tablespoons unsalted butter, room temperature
6 Tablespoons sugar
2 large egg yolks
2 Tablespoons softened crème cheese
1 teaspoon almond extract
¼ teaspoon vanilla extract
¼ teaspoon nutmeg
¼ teaspoon finely chopped parsley
¼ cup sliced almonds, finely ground

Directions

Cream the butter and sugar in a small bowl with a wooden spoon until light and fluffy.

Add the egg yolks, one at time, beating well after each addition.

Add crème cheese.

Beat.

Add almond extract, vanilla extract, nutmeg, parsley, and ground almonds.

Mix well.

Butterfly Butter

This can be slow and tedious, but well worth the effort.

Ingredients:

4 cups white-radish "Butterfly Wings" (See Directions)
⅛ cup clarified butter and savory salt (to taste), strained through cheesecloth.
1 large mint leaf
¼ teaspoon edible glitter (http://www.lusterdust.com/ludubycsa.html); we prefer the translucent white glitter for best effect.
¼ teaspoon Hawaiian Spice

Directions:

Peel white radishes.

Slice them thin as thinnest rice paper until you have 4 cups.

Soak slices in a large bowl of *very* icy water.

Once the slices begin to curl, caress each so it curls separately.

Once "wings" have curled, drain, and add clarified butter with savory salt.

Place mint leaf on soup, salad or any other dish.

Place wings on mint leaf.

Dust with edible glitter.

NOTE: if you want this sweeter, blend one teaspoon of powdered sugar in with the edible glitter before "dusting".

Sprinkle with Hawaiian Spice.

Caramelized Onions

Some things you must really learn how to do, because they're a basic part of some recipes. Even with the unique ingredients we use in our book's recipes, other things are just tried-and-true common sense.

Caramelizing brings out the natural flavor of onion(s) and changes their chemical balance to make them more stomach-friendly for those who find them unpalatable when raw. We use caramelized onions in lots of recipes. The key is in blending them with other flavors.

Caramelized onions are important to stews, soups, casseroles, and are delicious on toast points.

Ingredients:

Onions (you pick the number)
A few drops of oil
Clarified butter (See Recipe for Clarified Butter)
A wiggle (1/16 teaspoon) of NapaStyle® gray sea salt
A wiggle (1/16 teaspoon) of pepper
A wiggle (1/16 teaspoon) of sugar (if you just *have* to have sugar)
A drop or two of water, white wine, or beer,

Directions:

Boil onion(s) for about one minute to loosen skin and reduce watering of your eyes.

Peel and chop boiled onion(s).

NOTE: Split your onion(s) in half for easy chopping. Place half of an onion, cut side down, on a clean, flat cutting surface, and then chop.

In a large sauté pan, medium-high temperature, add your butter and a few drops of oil.

Add onion(s) and stir until they are coated with oil and butter.

Continue to stir, careful not to burn onion(s).

Add a pinch of salt (this will increase the speed of cooking, by taking away some of the moisture through rapid evaporation).

Add pepper and sugar.

Continue to stir but allow some of the onions to stick to the bottom of the pan (yes!) while onions continue to darken.

Add a drop or two of water, white wine, or beer, depending on your taste, to keep all of the onions from sticking, and loosening those that have.

Remove from heat when your desired degree of caramelization has occurred.

Chili Butter

Ingredients:

½ cup dark beer (or cabernet sauvignon wine)
1 cup cream cheese
2 cups clarified butter
1 Tablespoon Worcestershire® sauce
1 Tablespoon minced garlic
1 Tablespoon dried oregano
2 teaspoons ground cumin
2 teaspoons hot pepper sauce
1 teaspoon dried basil
1 teaspoon NapaStyle® gray sea salt
1 teaspoon ground black pepper
1 teaspoon cayenne pepper
1 teaspoon paprika
1 teaspoon white sugar
2 Tablespoons wheat flour
2 Tablespoons oat bran

Directions

Blend beer, cream cheese, and butter.

Add remaining ingredients.

Blend.

Refrigerate overnight.

Re-blend, before serving, if it has begun to separate.

Clarified Butter

Ingredients:

2½ cups of butter

Directions:

In a sauce pan, over a very low heat, place your butter.

Let butter melt slowly (don't play with it, just let it separate into the following three layers: foam, butterfat, water, and milk solids).

Skim off the foam.

Ladle out the butter fat (clarified butter)

Discard water and milk solids.

Or freeze the mixture and carve off the unusable top and bottom layers.

This makes about 2 cups of clarified butter.

Cranberry/Pinot-Noir Sauce

Ingredients:

2 cups whole cranberries
½ cup white sugar
½ cup water
1 cup firmly-packed brown sugar
1 cup pinot noir wine
1 teaspoon Mexican Spice
2 teaspoons hot Chinese mustard

Directions:

In a medium saucepan, combine cranberries, sugar, and water.

Bring to a boil.

Reduce heat.

Let simmer until cranberries are tender, stirring.

Add brown sugar, pinot noir wine, Mexican Spice, and Chinese mustard.

Stir.

Simmer 5 minutes, stirring often.

Remove from heat.

Honey Lemon Butter

Ingredients:

1 Tablespoon olive oil
¼ cup lemon zest
2 cups clarified butter
1 cup Greek honey-flavored yogurt

Directions:

In olive oil, scorch (brown) lemon zest.

Add clarified butter.

Fold in yogurt.

Refrigerate at least 24 hours.

Stir well before using.

Meringue

This can be used for pie or as an additional ingredient in other garnishes.

Ingredients:

4 egg whites
1 pinch cream of tartar
2 Tablespoons sugar

Directions:

Drop egg whites and cream of tartar in a bowl.

Whisk until soft peaks form.

Gradually add sugar and continue beating until stiff peaks re-form.

Pear Cream

Good on fruit soups and floating on most hot teas.

Ingredients:

One cup real cream
½ cup puréed pears (peeled and cored)
⅛ teaspoon pure vanilla extract
A dash (1/16 teaspoon) of nutmeg

Directions

Pour all ingredients into a bowl.

Whip until cream achieves high peaks.

Freeze until ready to serve.

Serve by the rounded teaspoon.

Picante

Ingredients:

1 large white onion
1 fresh jalapeño pepper
6 medium-sized ripe tomatoes
6 Tablespoons vegetable oil
1 teaspoon salt

¼ teaspoon granulated sugar
1 Tablespoon fresh, crushed cilantro

Directions:

Remove skin from onion.

Dime-size cube onion.

Remove stem from jalapeño and tomatoes.

NOTE: Keeping the jalapeño whole will reduce the "heat" aspects of the dish.

Cube (dime-size) the jalapeño and tomatoes.

In large frying pan, preheat the oil to medium temperature.

Add onions and sauté for about 10 minutes (or until tender, but *not* brown).

Add the remaining ingredients.

Turn heat to medium-low.

Simmer for about 10 minutes.

Remove jalapeño.

Pinked Butter

This doesn't store well; so, plan accordingly. If you're making something special just for yourself, quarter the recipe.

Pairs well with yellow/white dishes (i.e. lemon gelatin, or white asparagus).

Ingredients:

1 cup softened cream cheese
1 cup clarified butter
¼ cup dry red wine
½ cup Bing cherries, seeded, peeled, and finely chopped

Directions:

Combine cream cheese and clarified butter.

Whip.

Add wine and cherries.

Whip until nicely smooth, somewhat thick, pinkish color, and with pink bits.

Raisin Cream

Great on pie, ice-cream, or just served on salt-free crackers.

Ingredients:

1 cup heavy cream
⅛ teaspoon almond extract
A dash (1/16 teaspoon) of cinnamon

½ cup raisins, finely chopped

Directions:

Whip cream until it forms stiff peaks.

Fold in almond extract, cinnamon, and raisins.

Freeze until ready to serve.

Serve by rounded teaspoon.

Savory Butter

Ingredients:

½ teaspoon herbs
1 cup clarified butter

Directions:

Add whatever your chosen herb to clarified butter.

Stir.

Shrimp Cream

Can be rolled in various leafy vegetables, like butter lettuce, or served on savory toast points (see Savory Toast Points).

Ingredients:

Roux (See Recipe for Basic Roux)
1½ cups warmed milk
3 cups de-veined fresh baby shrimp, crushed, chopped, and

   strained
⅔ cup heavy cream
9 Tablespoons of dry white wine, preferably Sherry (or Riesling)
1 cup mozzarella cheese, shredded
1 Tablespoon lemon zest
½ teaspoon tarragon
½ teaspoon white pepper

Directions:

Add warmed milk to roux.

Stir.

Continue to cook over medium heat, stirring constantly, until sauce begins to thicken.

Add shrimp.

Stir.

Simmer, stirring constantly, over very low heat, until mixture thickens.

Add cream, sherry, cheese, zest, tarragon, white pepper.

Stir.

Cool.

Simple Syrup

Ingredients:

1 part water
2 parts sugar

Directions:

Bring water to a boil.

Add and dissolve sugar, stirring constantly; don't over boil or it will turn gluey.

Remove from heat and allow to thicken.

Cool.

Bottle.

Smooth Cream

Just about anything (white wine, cheeses, even herbs) can be blended with this for a unique taste. Careful, though, if you're out for "lemony", because juice can curdle the milk; best use zest. Great on pasta, potatoes, or vegetables.

Ingredients:

2 Tablespoons butter
2 Tablespoons all-purpose flour
1 cup heavy cream
1 cup melted cream cheese
A dash (1/16 teaspoon) of white pepper
A dash (1/16 teaspoon) of salt

Directions

In a pan on medium heat, melt butter.

Slowly add flour, and stir to form a paste.

Add cream,

Stir until smooth.

Add melted cream cheese.

Stir until smooth.

Turn up heat and bring mixture to a soft boil.

Stir constantly until you have a thick sauce.

Add pepper and salt.

Divide by 4 if you're cooking for yourself.

Spicy Dried Tomatoes

Not officially served in dollops, unless you, first, purée them with virgin olive oil, these make great garnish for all types of food. Actually, it's their umami (the scientific term for the taste of glutamates and nucleotides, now widely accepted as the fifth basic taste), that make these so yummy.

Ingredients:

10 Roma tomatoes
A dash (1/16 teaspoon) NapaStyle® gray sea salt
A dash (1/16 teaspoon) of white pepper

2 Tablespoons hot sauce
2 Tablespoons chili powder

Additional "things" needed:

Small drying table for outside.
A screen on which to place tomatoes.
Enough cheesecloth to cover tomatoes without touching them.
Drying screen with legs (squared-3D cover)
Good attitude.
Lots of patience.

Directions:

Slice tomatoes in 8 even slices; soak in hot sauce and chili.

Place on a drying screen.

NOTE: We have made a little 3D box out of screen about 4 inches tall.

Lightly sprinkle with NapaStyle® gray sea salt and spices and place in the hot sun until dry.

Properly ventilate (and keep bugs away) by covering with cheesecloth that doesn't touch the tomatoes.

Leave in sun every day (don't forget to bring them in each night) until tomatoes are dry, usually, about one week; although, in humid areas, it will be closer to 2 weeks.

12 fresh tomatoes give about one-ounce of dried.

Sunset Sauce

Ingredients:

1 Tablespoon brown sugar
2 Tablespoons roux (See Recipe for Basic Roux)
½ cup juice of one fresh orange
½ cup juice from fresh cherries
½ cup juice from a fresh lemon
½ cup juice from a fresh lime
2 Tablespoons butter
¼ teaspoon grated orange zest
¼ teaspoon grated lime zest
¼ teaspoon grated lemon zest
1 Tablespoon Riesling wine

Directions:

Combine brown sugar and roux in a saucepan.

Add juice, butter and zest.

Cook on medium heat, stirring constantly, until thickened.

Add wine.

Sweet Butter

Sweet Butter is just that...SWEET.

Ingredients:

1 cup heavy cream
1 cup clarified butter
¼ cup port wine

1 cup powdered sugar
¼ teaspoon pure vanilla extract

Directions:

In a bowl, whip heavy cream until stiff.

In separate bowl, whip clarified butter until frothy.

Blend cream, butter, port wine, powdered sugar, and vanilla extract.

Keep refrigerated.

Tomato Butter

Ingredients:

6 two-inch marigold heads, (Don't panic, they'll be dried and ground to a powder per directions)
¼ teaspoon paprika chili powder
¼ teaspoon poblano pepper (dried and ground)
A dash (1/16 teaspoon) of NapaStyle gray sea salt
1 Tablespoon flour
2 cups peeled and seeded red Roma tomatoes, mashed and puréed
½ cup cooled clarified butter

Directions:

Pull petals off the marigold heads, discard heads, and let petals dry; the humidity will determine how long the drying will take.

Rub dried petals between the palms of your hands to produce marigold powder.

Combine marigold powder, spices, and flour, and put to one side.

Slash skins of your tomatoes.

Drop tomatoes into boiling water for several seconds.

Remove tomatoes and peel.

Cut open tomatoes and remove seeds.

Slice tomatoes thin and sauté until brown.

Let tomatoes cool, then purée in a blender.

Combine paprika chili powder, pepper, and salt with tomatoes.

Stir.

Add clarified butter.

Whip until smooth.

Whisky Crème

Ingredients:

1 cup "Plain" Savory Crème (see Savory Crème, *minus herbs*)
1 cup clarified butter
½ teaspoon coconut essence
4 Tablespoons whisky

Directions:

Combine all ingredients.

Beat until smooth.

Keep refrigerated.

White Butter-Wine

This must be served within 15 minutes of making; so, plan accordingly. It will separate if not refrigerated. It's wonderful over fish, though, and can be used as dressing on green salads, aspic, or just to "spice up" something, or as a shrimp-dip.

Ingredients:

1 cup clarified butter
4 egg whites beat into a meringue—(see Meringue)
1 pinch of tartar
¼ cup sweet white Riesling

Directions:

In a bowl, beat clarified butter to a nice bubbly froth.

Gently fold in the meringue.

Slowly add tartar and wine.

You end up with a nice smooth somewhat-thick cream sauce.

White Sauce

Ingredients:

3 Tablespoons roux (See Recipe for Basic Roux)
2 cups fresh heavy cream, warmed to room temperature
1 wiggle (1/16 teaspoon) of salt

A dash (1/16 teaspoon) nutmeg
1 wiggle (1/16 teaspoon) white pepper

Directions:

Put a pot over low heat.

Add roux.

Cook and whisk until slightly golden.

Whisk in cream, a little at a time, being careful not to let lumps form. Whisking regularly, bring to a boil and continue cooking until thickened.

Remove pot from the heat.

If there are any lumps, strain, using a cheese cloth or strainer.

Add salt, nutmeg and pepper.

Stir and let cool.

HORS D'ŒUVRES

Bacon-Wrapped Dates

Ingredients:

1 pound large dried dates
Several slices Munster Cheese
1 pound smoked bacon

Directions:

Wrap each individual date with a strip of Munster Cheese.

Cut bacon strips in half.

Fry bacon strips in large frying pan. Blot bacon dry.

Wrap one hot bacon strip around each date and cheese.

Affix each bacon-strip to date and cheese with toothpick.

Bite the Beef

Ingredients:

1 pound beef tips, cut into ½-inch cubes
2 Tablespoons butter
1 teaspoon Italian spice
1 cup dried tomatoes, chopped
½ cup fresh mango, puréed

Directions:

Sauté beef tips in butter.

Season with Italian spice and dried tomatoes.

Strain, then pat with paper towels, to reduce residual butter.

Return to pan.

Add puréed mango.

Stir until hot.

Remove from heat.

Bourbon Orange Glaze Shrimp Babies

Ingredients:

1½ cups shredded coconut
1 pound fresh cocktail shrimp
6 teaspoons bourbon
Juice from 2 squeezed oranges
½ teaspoon orange extract

1 Tablespoon brown sugar
3 Tablespoons butter
1 teaspoon ground ginger

Directions:

Pre heat broiler to 350° degrees.

Broil shredded coconut until brown; do not leave unattended as it burns quickly.

Remove coconut from broiler.

Broil shrimp for 7 minutes.

Remove shrimp from broiler.

Combine broiled shrimp and broiled browned coconut; set aside.

In a small saucepan, add bourbon, orange juice, orange extract, brown sugar, butter, and ginger.

Simmer until thickened.

Pour over coconut and shrimp.

Spoon into glass serving dish.

Refrigerate.

Serve with a side of cream cheese (or some other garnish) and water crackers.

Chunky Artichoke Spread

Ingredients

2 cups marinated artichoke hearts, drained
2 cups Neufchatel cheese
1 cup fresh shredded Parmesan cheese
½ cup cream cheese
¼ cup sun-dried tomatoes softened with olive oil
¼ cup green onions, diced

Directions:

Preheat oven to 350° degrees.

Combine all ingredients in a baking dish and stir well.

Bake 30 minutes, or until golden & bubbly.

Serve with bread sticks, crackers, French bread, or apple slices.

Crab & Cucumber Puffs

Ingredients:

Pâté à Choux, unbaked (See Recipe for Pâté à Choux)
1 package cream cheese, softened
1 Tablespoon heavy cream
1 Tablespoon horseradish
¼ teaspoon ground black pepper
1 teaspoon oriental spice
4 green onions, diced
½ pound fresh crabmeat, rinsed, drained and chopped fine
Cucumber slices, one per puff
½ cup sliced almonds

½ teaspoon paprika

Directions:

Make Pâté à Choux as directed.

Put Pâté à Choux in pastry piping bag.

Pipe bite-sized dollops onto a cookie sheet.

Bake according to pastry cooking directions, and set aside.

Let cool.

Slice cooled puffs in half, width-wise.

Blend cream cheese in a medium bowl until smooth.

Stir in heavy cream, horseradish, black pepper, oriental spice, onions, and crabmeat.

Place one cucumber slice on the bottom slice of each puff.

Spoon crabmeat mixture onto cucumber slice.

Top crabmeat mixture with almonds.

Put top slice back on bottom slice of puff.

Sprinkle with paprika.

Crottin & Coconut on Baguettes

Ingredients:

2 packages Crottin cheese (light citrus flavor)
2 Tablespoons cream cheese, soft
1 cup sweet coconut, browned under the broiler
1 teaspoon Hawaiian spice
1 wiggle (1/16 teaspoon) NapaStyle® gray sea salt
A dash (1/16 teaspoon) pepper
Baguette slices

Directions:

Blend all ingredients, except baguette slices.

Refrigerate.

Spread on baguette slices.

Killer Compote

Be forewarned that though Durian fruit is fabulous-tasting, it is foul-smelling.

Ingredients:

½ cup chokeberries, cut in half
½ cup serviceberries, cut in half
½ cup huckleberries
½ cup cloudberries, cut in half
½ cup horned melon, de-seeded, peeled, chopped
½ cup Durian
Monstera deliciosa, pull individual fruits one by one
¼ cup Simple Syrup (see Recipe for Simple Syrup)

Directions:

Gently combine all ingredients but Simple Syrup.

Add Simple Syrup.

Gently mix.

Chill.

Serve on toast points, topped with any sweet crèmes or creams.

Pungent Garlic Dip and Apricots

Ingredients:

1 package cream cheese, softened
⅛ teaspoon NapaStyle® gray sea salt
2 drops hot sauce
3 garlic cloves, chopped and broiled
Dried apricots, cut open like a baked potato, de-pitted
Italian parsley

Directions:

Blend cream cheese, NapaStyle® gray sea salt, and hot sauce.

Put mixture in pastry piping bag.

Make florets inside the hollows of cut-open apricots.

Garnish with Italian parsley.

Chill for 1 hour before serving.

Smoky Cheese Ball

Ingredients:

1 Tablespoon Liquid Smoke
2 packages cream cheese, room temperature
8 ounces shredded sharp Cheddar cheese
2 packages Gourmandise cheese
2 teaspoons garlic, finely minced
1 cup pecans, puréed
1 cup sliced almonds

Directions:

Blend all ingredients, except sliced almonds, in a bowl.

Roll into round balls and set aside.

Toast almonds in the oven.

Roll cheese balls in almonds until balls are covered.

Serve with toast points or crackers.

Spiced Ham Boats

Ingredients:

Pâté à Choux, unbaked (See Recipe for Pâté à Choux and halve it)
½ pound deli ham, minced
2 teaspoons paprika
1 Tablespoon hot sauce (additional if desired)
2 Tablespoons hot yellow mustard
1 eight-ounce package cream cheese at room temperature

1 cup extra-sharp yellow cheddar cheese, shredded
¼ cup small black olives, sliced into thin rounds
Handful of flat-leaf parsley

Directions:

Put Pâté à Choux in pastry piping bag.

On to baking sheet, pipe dough, in the shape of little 2"-long "boats".

Bake according to Pâté à Choux cooking directions, and set aside.

Blend ham, paprika, hot sauce, hot yellow mustard, cream cheese, cheddar cheese, and olives, in a food processor to chunky consistency, not purée.

Cut off the top third off each little pastry boat, and fill with chunky ingredients.

Replace the top of the boat.

Tuck a little piece of parsley on either side of each boat to imitate oars.

Stuffed Mushrooms with Quail

Remember that mushrooms can be stuffed with almost anything.

Ingredients:

Pinch of salt
1 pound shitake mushrooms
Quail, cooked and separated from bone

1 Tablespoon butter
3 Tablespoons NapaStyle® gray sea salt
3 Tablespoons ground white pepper
3 Tablespoons coarsely ground black pepper
2 Tablespoons tawny port
½ cup crumbled goat cheese

Directions:

Fill a medium pot with water.

Bring to a boil, and add a pinch of salt.

Remove stems from mushroom caps.

Drop mushroom caps in boiling water for exactly 15 seconds.

Remove mushroom caps from boiling water.

Refrigerate.

Chop quail into small pieces.

Add butter, NapaStyle® gray sea salt, white pepper, and black pepper.

Sauté.

Add port and reduce.

Spoon mixture into individual mushroom caps.

Sprinkle with goat cheese.

Broil for 5 minutes or until goat cheese is melted and slightly brown.

Tiny Ravioli

Ingredients:

Ravioli dough (See Recipe for Ravioli-Tortellini Pasta Dough)
1 pound ground chicken
1½ cups fresh spinach
5 Tablespoons grated Parmesan cheese
1¼ Tablespoons dried parsley
¼ cup olive oil
1 large egg
½ teaspoon garlic salt
1 pinch black pepper
2 egg whites
2 Tablespoons water

Directions:

Cut ravioli dough into 1" x 1" squares, and put to one side.

Lightly oil large skillet and place over medium-high heat.

Stir in ground chicken and cook to crumbling and evenly browned.

Drain excess grease.

Add spinach and cook until wilted.

Remove from heat.

Cool 10 minutes.

Transfer mixture to bowl.

Add the Parmesan cheese, parsley, olive oil, large egg, garlic salt, and pepper.

Mix well.

Run through grinder until smooth and puréed.

Spoon (or melon-ball scoop) a teaspoon into centers of every other pasta square.

In a bowl, using a fork, emulsify 2 egg whites and 2 Tablespoons water.

Lightly brush egg-white wash around the edges of each filled ravioli square.

Place an empty ravioli square over each filled egg-washed pasta square.

Use fingers to press firmly around all edges to seal pasta squares.

In a very large pot, bring salted water to boil.

Cook ravioli in boiling water for 3-4 minutes, careful not to overcook.

Drain carefully.

Serve with favorite sauce, or grated Parmesan cheese and black pepper.

PÂTÉS

American Teen Pâté

Ingredients:

1 pound hot dogs, peeled and ground
2 cups water
¼ cup hot mustard
¼ cup ketchup
¼ teaspoon NapaStyle® gray sea salt
¼ teaspoon ground white pepper
3 Tablespoons flour

Directions:

In saucepan, combine ground hot dogs and water.

Bring to a boil, reduce heat to low, and cover.

Simmer for about 20 minutes, or until hot dogs are cooked.

Remove from heat, drain.

Process cooked hot dogs in a blender until smooth.

Add mustard, ketchup, salt, white pepper, and flour.

In short bursts, blend until smooth; if dry, add more ketchup.

Using wax paper, roll ingredient into a tube.

Refrigerate for at least 2 hours.

Serve thinly sliced on tiny hamburger buns.

Apricot Pâté

Ingredients:

1½ cups dried apricots, chopped into very small cubes
2 cups boiling water
¾ cup Riesling wine
½ cup water
¼ cup sugar
½ orange zest
1½ teaspoons dark rum
A dash (1/16 teaspoon) of ground oregano
1 Tablespoon flour
1 Tablespoon plain yogurt (preferably Greek yogurt)

Directions:

Place apricots in bowl with 2 cups boiling water for 10 minutes.

Drain and set aside.

Combine wine, ½-cup water, sugar, orange zest, dark rum, and oregano in a small saucepan.

Cook on medium-high until sugar has melted.

Reduce heat and simmer until all liquid becomes syrupy.

Slowly add apricots to syrup.

Cook until apricots are very soft (about 15 minutes).

Remove from heat.

Let cool completely.

Add flour and yogurt.

In food processor, purée until mixture is smooth (add drops of water if too dry).

Refrigerate.

Asparagus and White Grape Pâté

Ingredients:

½ cup grapes, peeled, seeded, and finely chopped
1 bunch asparagus, fresh
2 Tablespoons flour
½ cup pecans, ground
½ cup roasted pine nuts, chopped
4 ounces cream cheese, softened
1 small garlic clove, finely chopped
⅛ teaspoon clove, ground
¼ teaspoon white pepper
1 Tablespoon heavy cream

Directions:

Purée grapes and put aside.

Lightly simmer asparagus until slightly limp.

Drain asparagus and put in blender.

Add puréed grapes.

Using short spurts, blend until smooth.

Add flour, pecans, and pine nuts.

Blend.

Add cream cheese, garlic, glove, and pepper.

Use heavy cream as smoothing agent.

Blend.

Line small decorative molds, or small bowls, with plastic food wrap, or with butter and flour.

Press mixture into the molds or bowls, and level with a knife.

Refrigerate.

Chocolate Liver Pâté

Ingredients:

1 pound chicken liver
3 cups water
5 Tablespoons cooking sherry
¾ cup butter, softened
¼ teaspoon NapaStyle® gray sea salt
¼ teaspoon white pepper, ground
⅛ teaspoon mace, ground
½ teaspoon cardamom

½ cup unsweetened chocolate, ground

Directions

In a saucepan, combine chicken livers with water.

Bring to a boil, reduce heat to low, and cover.

Simmer for about 20 minutes, or until liver is cooked and tender.

Remove from heat, and drain.

Trim any hard fatty portions of the liver.

Blend cooked livers until smooth.

Add sherry, butter, salt, pepper, mace, cardamom, and chocolate, all in short blender bursts, until smooth; if dry add more sherry.

Using wax paper, roll ingredient into a tube.

Refrigerate for at least 2 hours.

Serve sliced thinly with crepes.

Crab Pâté

Ingredients

14 ounces fresh crabmeat, chopped very fine
2 teaspoons white wine
2 teaspoons lemon juice
½ teaspoon Worcestershire sauce
1 cup lemon-flavored Greek yogurt

8 ounces cream cheese, soft
⅛ teaspoon salt
⅛ teaspoon curry powder
1 Tablespoon fresh onion, grated
½ teaspoon fresh garlic, grated

Directions

Purée crabmeat, white wine, lemon juice, Worcestershire® sauce, and yogurt, to a very fine texture.

Scrape out with rubber spatula, and add remaining ingredients.

Mix well.

Refrigerate.

Cucumber Pâté

There are two ways to begin.

One:

Peel 6 cucumbers and dry their peels in a dehydrator.

Grind the dried peel into fine particles.

Refrigerate until making Cucumber Pâté.

If you start that way, you're a bona-fide foodie. If you can't go to the bother, then leave out this step and proceed to...

Two:

Ingredients

1 egg white
6 cucumbers, peeled, seeded and cubed
2 cups cream cheese, softened
2 Tablespoons pinot blanc wine
1 wiggle (1/16 teaspoon) NapaStyle® gray sea salt
2 sprigs parsley, chopped fine
⅛ teaspoon white pepper
2 shallots, peeled and finely chopped
1 Tablespoon dried cucumber peel (see above)
1 teaspoon horseradish
1 wiggle (1/16 teaspoon) dill

Directions

Beat the egg white until stiff and put to one side.

Purée the cucumbers.

Slowly add the cream cheese, wine and remaining spices...other than cucumber peel—to the purée.

Fold in the stiffened egg white.

Gently, fold in the ground cucumber peel (or not; see above).

Olive & Truffle Pâté

Ingredients:

8 roasted garlic cloves, unpeeled
1 cup Fontina cheese, cubed

¼ cup cream cheese
2 cups Kalamata olives, pitted (or use your favorite olive if you prefer)
1 cup sautéed truffles
⅛ teaspoon ground clove
¼ cup olive oil

Directions:

Preheat oven to 350 degrees F.

Tightly wrap garlic cloves in aluminum foil and bake 30 minutes.

Remove from oven, open foil, and let garlic cloves rest about 10 minutes until cool enough to handle.

Pinch each clove from the root end to squeeze garlic pulp into a small bowl; set aside for later.

Melt Fontina cheese in a double-boiler over simmering (not boiling) water, stirring until smooth.

Blend in the cream cheese.

Using a blender, purée olives, truffles, garlic, ground clove, and olive oil about 15 seconds.

Add melted cheese and blend about 10 more seconds until combined.

Refrigerate at least 2 hours.

Before serving, let pâté rest for 30 minutes at room temperature.

Pea 'n' Pea Pâté

Yes, chickpeas do come in a can, but we always use fresh "anything," whenever possible, by way of maximizing nutrients and flavor.

For this recipe, then, fresh *dried* chickpeas are requested; find them packaged, or in bulk, at your local grocery story. Be sure, though, to check the date on the package to assure their freshness.

Ingredients

3 cups chickpeas, fresh, dried
½ cup sweet potatoes
½ cup sweet peas, fresh
1 clove garlic, toasted and ground
1 wiggle (1/16 teaspoon) turmeric
½ teaspoon cumin, powdered
⅛ teaspoon of clove, grown
1 wiggle (1/16 teaspoon) NapaStyle® gray sea salt

Directions:

Toast chickpeas by sautéing them in a pan until they're slightly colored; keep the pan moving so you don't scorch them.

Put them in a pot and cover with plain cold water (*no salt*); let set for 24 hours.

Cook chickpeas for around 1-2 hours, WITHOUT salt, until soft but not falling apart.

Once cooked, chickpeas should have a creamy texture; remove meat by "squeezing" out of and discarding skins.

Put cooked and skinned chickpeas to one side.

Peel and cook the sweet potato, and put to one side.

Peel and cook the sweet peas, in a light boil.

In a blender, purée chickpeas, potato, and sweet peas.

Add remaining ingredients and spices, including (now that all is cooked) salt.

Blend

Refrigerate.

Pineapple Ham Pâté

Ingredients:

1 pound ham, cubed
½ cup cherries, peeled, seeded, and chopped
½ cup finely fresh pineapple, chopped
Green onions (to taste)
3 ounces cream cheese, softened
1 small white onion, finely chopped
½ cup walnuts, ground
¼ teaspoon sage, ground
¼ teaspoon white pepper
1 Tablespoon heavy cream

Directions:

Using a blender, and short spurts, purée ham to very fine; if you use a grinder, push the ham through at least twice; put to one side.

Purée cherries and pineapple; put to one side.

Purée green onions; put to one side.

In a bowl, blend cream cheese, white onion, and nuts.

Add prepared ham.

Blend.

Add puréed green onions.

Blend.

Add puréed fruit.

Blend.

Add sage and pepper.

Use heavy cream as smoothing agent.

Blend.

Line small decorative molds, or small bowls, with plastic food wrap, or with butter and flour.

Press mixture into the molds or bowls, and level with a knife.

Refrigerate.

Red Wine Grape Pâté

This is good to serve to vegetarians.

Ingredients:

1 Tablespoon olive oil
1 small onion, finely chopped
1 clove of garlic, crushed
⅛ teaspoon thyme
½ cup red wine
½ cup vegetable stock
3 Tablespoon crumbs from French bread
3 Tablespoons oat bran
1 Tablespoon brandy
6 Tablespoons peeled, seeded, and puréed red grapes
2 teaspoons soy sauce
1 wiggle (1/16 teaspoon) NapaStyle® gray sea salt
1 wiggle (1/16 teaspoon) white pepper
Sprig of Italian parsley

Directions:

Prepared a pâté mold, and set aside.

In a saucepan, heat oil.

Add onion, garlic, dried thyme.

Cook until ingredients are soft.

Add red wine and vegetable stock.

Bring to a boil.

Remove from heat.

Stir in the breadcrumbs, oat bran, brandy, grape purée, and soy sauce.

Salt and pepper to taste.

Cook over gentle heat until thickened.

Pour into prepared mold.

Refrigerate.

Unmold for serving.

Garnish with sprig of Italian parsley.

Strawberry Pâté

Ingredients:

16 seedless strawberries
16 ounces cream cheese, softened
8 ounces unsalted butter, softened
1 cup powdered sugar, sifted
1 teaspoon vanilla
2 Tablespoons white rum
1 teaspoon flour
A wiggle (1/16 teaspoon) NapaStyle® gray sea salt

Directions

In a blender, purée strawberries and set aside.

Whip cream cheese, butter, and sugar until light and fluffy.

Add vanilla, rum, flour, NapaStyle® gray sea salt, and strawberries.

Beat until smooth.

Serve cold.

Vegetable Pâté

Ingredients:

1 envelope unflavored gelatin
½ cup cold water
1 Tablespoon butter
1 small onion, chopped
½ pound diced mushrooms
1 cup fresh green beans
½ cup walnuts, chopped
½ cup parsley, chopped
1 Tablespoon lemon juice
1 teaspoon hot sauce
¼ teaspoon dried thyme
1 wiggle (1/16 teaspoon) fresh nutmeg, grated
Salt and freshly ground pepper to taste
1 teaspoon Vegetable Spice (see Vegetable Spice)

Directions:

Sprinkle the gelatin over the water in a small saucepan and soak for 5 minutes.

Heat over very low heat, stirring constantly, until the gelatin is completely dissolved; set aside for later.

Heat butter in a large skillet over moderate heat and sauté onion and mushrooms until tender but not brown, about 5 minutes.

Add the green beans and cook for 5 minutes.

Process cooked vegetables, gelatin, and remaining ingredients in a blender until puréed.

Pour into a 3-cup mold and refrigerate for at least 2 hours.

Unmold and serve with crackers.

BREADS-ROLLS-CREPES-CHIPS-PIE CRUSTS-THICKENERS-DOUGH

Basic Crepes

Ingredients:

1 cup flour
2 eggs
½ cup heavy cream
½ cup water
¼ teaspoon NapaStyle® gray sea salt
2 Tablespoons butter, melted

Directions:

In a large mixing bowl, whisk eggs while slowly adding cream and water

Add salt and butter, and; beat until smooth.

Use a coated six-inch frying pan (not too hot or crepes will burn), and scoop batter into pan, using approximately ¼ cup for each crepe.

Jiggle pan gently, with a circular motion that spreads the batter evening across the bottom of the pan.

Cook until light brown (about 2 minutes).

Flip, if you can; if you can't, loosen with a rubber spatula, turn, and cook the other side. Serve hot.

Basic Roux

This is a basic thickening for sauces and soups.

Ingredients:

4 Tablespoons butter
4 Tablespoons flour

Directions:

Melt butter in small sauce pan.

Slowly add flour, stirring constantly for about 3 minutes.

The roux is done when the flour smells like bread.

Bearlee Fruit Bread

Ingredients:

½ cup pine nuts, coarsely chopped
1½ cups dried cherries, coarsely chopped
1½ cups dried apricots, coarsely chopped
1½ cups dried cranberries, coarsely chopped
1½ cups frozen blueberries, coarsely chopped
¾ cup yellow raisins
¼ cup apple juice

3½ cups all-purpose white flour
1 Tablespoon baking powder
1 teaspoon baking soda
½ teaspoon salt
1 large egg
2 large egg whites
½ cup sugar
⅔ cup nonfat plain yogurt
3 Tablespoons hazelnut oil (or canola oil)
1 Tablespoon grated lemon zest
1 teaspoon pure vanilla extract

Directions:

Preheat oven to 350° F.

Lightly butter and flour two 9" x 5" loaf pans; put aside until later.

In a shallow pan, sauté pine nuts, in a pan, until golden brown and fragrant; set aside to cool.

In a small saucepan, combine fruits and juice.

Bring to a simmer.

Remove from heat and let stand for 10 minutes.

Transfer to a food processor and process to a chunky purée; set aside for later.

In a large bowl, whisk flour, baking powder, soda, and salt.

In another large bowl, whisk egg, egg whites, sugar, yogurt, oil, lemon zest, and vanilla.

Combine fruit and juice purée with dry ingredients.

Fold in whisked egg, egg whites, sugar, yogurt, oil, lemon zest, and vanilla mixture.

Fold in nuts.

Pop the batter into oiled and lightly floured pan, smoothing the top.

Bake for 50-60 minutes, or until the top is golden brown (a skewer inserted in the center should come out clean).

Let cool in the pan for 10 minutes, then loosen edges and invert the loaf onto a wire rack to remove.

Cool.

Butter Crust for Pies or Casseroles

This crust can be used for many dishes; so, don't hesitate to add your favorite herbs, flowers, vegetables, or fruit to enhance it; just add an equal weight in liquid to keep the recipe's consistency.

Ingredients:

2½ cups all-purpose flour, plus extra for rolling
1 teaspoon salt
1 teaspoon sugar
8 ounces butter, unsalted, very-cold, cut into ½ inch cubes
6-8 Tablespoons ice water
Clarified butter (See Recipe for Clarified Butter) for final basting
   (See Recipe for Clarified Butter)

Directions *for Pies:*

Pre-heat oven to 425-450° F., depending upon your location and your oven's predictability.

Combine flour, salt, and sugar in a food processor.

Add butter and mix in 6-8 short bursts, until coarse meal, with pea-size pieces of butter.

Add ice water a Tablespoon at a time at a time, mixing in spurts until mixture begins to clump; if you pinch crumbly dough and it holds, it's ready; if dough doesn't hold, add a little more water and mix again.

Place dough on a clean surface.

Gently shape into 2 round loaves (don't over-knead; you should be able to still see little bits of butter).

Sprinkle a little flour around the discs, and wrap each disc in plastic wrap.

Refrigerate for 24-48 hours.

Remove one loaf from the refrigerator, and let sit at room temperature for a few minutes.

Use a rolling pin, on a lightly floured surface, to form dough into a 12-inch circle; about ⅛ of an inch thick; if necessary, add a few sprinkles of flour under the dough to keep it from sticking.

Place into a buttered and floured 9-inch pie plate, and gently press the dough down to line the bottom and sides of the plate.

Use kitchen scissors to trim the excess dough to within ½ inch of the edge of the plate.

Add filling; put to one side until later.

Remove the second loaf from the refrigerator, and let sit at room temperature for a few minutes.

Use a rolling pin, on a lightly floured surface, to form dough into a 12-inch circle; about $\frac{1}{8}$ an inch thick; if necessary, add a few sprinkles of flour under the dough to keep it from sticking.

Gently place this second dough on top of the pie filling, and inch to seal bottom and top crusts firmly together.

Trim excess dough with kitchen shears, leaving $\frac{3}{4}$-inch overhang.

Fold the edge of the top piece of dough over and under the edge of the bottom piece of dough, pressing together.

Flute resulting edges, using thumb and forefinger (or press with fork tongs).

Score the top of the pie with four 2-inch long cuts (or cut a design or picture).

Directions *for Casseroles:*

Make 3 loaves: with one, line the casserole dish, and add half your filling.

With two, provide a middle layer, and add the other half of your filling.

With three, cover the filling, and seal first layer with the third, and bake.

Five Cheese Bread Twists

Ingredients:

6 Tablespoons butter (or margarine), softened
1 garlic clove, minced
⅛ teaspoon pepper
3 Tablespoons heavy cream
½ cup shredded Cheddar cheese
½ cup shredded Monterey Jack cheese
½ cup shredded Mozzarella cheese
½ cup crumbled Ricotta cheese
½ cup shredded Parmesan cheese
½ jalapeño pepper, chopped fine
½ sweet banana pepper, chopped fine
1¼ cup all-purpose flour

Directions:

In a mixing bowl, combine butter, garlic, and pepper; beat until light and fluffy.

Stir in heavy cream, cheeses (save a bit of Parmesan for later sprinkling), Jalapeño, and Sweet Banana peppers.

Gradually add flour, mixing thoroughly (if too dry, use a few drops of water).

Divide dough into 20 pieces.

Roll each piece into a ten-inch tube.

Cut each tube in half, lengthwise, and twist together, NOT pinching the ends.

Place one inch apart on ungreased baking sheet.

Bake in preheated at 375° over for about 12 minutes (or until golden brown).

Sprinkle saved Parmesan cheese over the tops while hot.

Put on cooling racks.

Mini Feta Cheese Curls

Ingredients:

8 cups all-purpose flour
4 cups crumbled feta cheese
¾ cup minced cherry peppers
8 Tablespoons white sugar
1½ teaspoons salt
½ teaspoon chopped garlic cloves
½ teaspoon fresh chives
½ teaspoon ground clove
2 cups hot water
3 one-fourth-of-an-ounce packages active dry yeast
4 Tablespoons vegetable oil

Directions:

In one large bowl, combine 7 cups of flour, feta, cherry peppers, 7 Tablespoons sugar and salt.

Mix well.

In a separate bowl, combine water, yeast and remaining 1 Tablespoon sugar.

Let sit 10 minutes.

Stir until all yeast is dissolved.

Add the oil to the liquid mixture.

Mix well.

Add half of the liquid mixture to the flour mixture.

Mix.

Add remaining liquid mixture to dough.

Knead until flour is thoroughly saturated.

Put onto lightly floured surface and knead until smooth and elastic, about 10-12 minutes, adding only enough additional flour to achieve the proper consistency.

Place in a large oiled bowl, turning dough to make sure its outside surface is oiled.

Cover with a dry towel and let stand in a warm place until doubled in size, about 1 hour.

Punch down dough.

Bake at 325° F until dark brown and done, about 40 minute to an hour, rotating the pans after 25 minutes for more even browning.

Remove from pan as soon as bread will easily lift out, after about 5 to 10 minutes.

Let cool about 1 hour before serving.

NOTE: To Make Mini Breads: Use a rolling pin after first rise and punch-down to roll out the dough; then, put dough into a pastry bag without a tip. Squeeze out enough dough into an oiled and floured cupcake tin to fill each mold halfway. By working circles of dough in a mold, you'll end up with a lovely spring-shaped loaf. Cover with towel and allow to rise until almost doubled, about 45 minutes to 1 hour.

Nut and Grain Wheat Bread

Ingredients:

3 cups warm water
2 one-fourth-ounce packages active dry yeast
½ cup honey
8½ cups wheat flour (with possibility of up to 2½ cups more)
5 Tablespoons butter, melted
1 Tablespoon salt
1½ cups almonds, walnuts and pecans, very finely chopped
1½ cups oat bran
½ cup oatmeal

Directions:

In a large bowl, mix water, yeast, and honey.

Add 6 cups wheat flour, and stir to combine.

Let dough set for 30 minutes, or until large and airy.

Mix in 3 Tablespoons melted butter, and salt.

Stir in remaining 2½ cups whole wheat flour.

Put on floured flat surface and knead until it pulls away from the surface, but isn't sticky to the touch. If you need additional flour to achieve this consistency, then add it.

Evenly fold in nuts, oat bran, and oatmeal; if mixture proves too dry, add more water.

Place in an oiled bowl, coating surface of the dough with oil.

Cover with a dishtowel and let rise in a warm place until doubled.

Punch down, and divide into 3 loaves.

Place each loaf in an oiled 9 x 5 inch loaf pan.

Let rise until dough tops the pan by approximately 1".

Bake at 350 degrees for 25-30 minutes; watching for a lovely light brown color.

Remove from oven.

Lightly brush the top of each loaf with remaining melted butter.

Cool.

Olé de Cerdo Adobado Pan

Ingredients:

1 cup onions, chopped
½ pound cooked pork roast
3 cups water
¼ ounce active dry yeast
¼ cup warm water
1 teaspoon sugar

3 cups unbleached flour
1½ cups barley flour (or whole wheat flour)
½ flat teaspoon nutmeg
½ flat Tablespoon cinnamon
½ flat teaspoon chervil
½ flat teaspoon fennel
½ flat teaspoon sage
½ flat teaspoon thyme
½ flat teaspoon coriander
½ flat teaspoon caraway seeds
1 teaspoon Mexican spices (see Recipe for Mexican Spice)
½ cup lukewarm milk
Pork broth
2 teaspoons salt

Directions:

In a large sauce pan, put chopped onions and pork in 3 cups of boiling water.

Turn to medium heat.

Cook until pork is done (about 3 hours).

Let cool.

Take pork out, drain, pull apart, and chop into 1-inch bites; set aside for later.

Take out onions, strain, and purée; set aside for later.

Strain the broth; set aside for later.

To ¼ cup of warm water, add sugar, and yeast.

Stir and let sit in a warm place until the yeast is bubbly &

doubles in volume; set aside for later.

In a large bowl, mix unbleached flour, barley flour, and spices.

Add dissolved yeast, and milk.

Add enough lukewarm broth to form stiff dough.

Using floured bread board, knead until the dough isn't sticky (10-15 minutes).

Fold in onion purée and meat.

Knead until thoroughly mixed.

Split dough into loaves.

Let rise for an hour.

Place in preheated 350° oven until baked (about 30 minutes).

Pâté à Choux (Puff Pastry)

Here is another one of those recipes Cecile "borrowed" from her Grammy.

Ingredients:

1 cup water
1 stick butter, unsalted
1 teaspoon sugar
½ teaspoon NapaStyle® gray sea salt
1 cup flour
5 large eggs

Directions:

Put the water, butter, sugar and salt into a sauce pan and bring to a rolling boil.

Remove the pan from the burner, and add cup of flour.

Stir with a wooden spoon until the dough forms a coherent "ball".

Return the pan to medium heat and cook for another minute, stirring constantly.

Remove from burner and place dough into mixing bowl.

Stir quickly with a heavy hand until dough has cooled.

Add eggs, one at a time, until the batter is smooth and shiny.

Put dough in pastry bag and squeeze onto baking sheet.

Place in preheated 400°, and bake until golden.

This is terrific for making, and baking, little "birds" and "animals" to put on sweet confections.

Ravioli-Tortellini Pasta Dough

This is another of Cecile's Gammy recipes. If you mess it up, fry it, top with any sweet garnish (See Recipes for Garnishes), and sprinkle with powdered sugar.

Ingredients:

4 eggs

⅞ pound fine white flour
Healthy pinch of salt

Directions:

Break eggs into a bowl; put aside until later.

Make mound of the flour on your work surface and scoop out a well in the middle.

Pour eggs into the hole.

Add salt.

Hand-work the eggs and the flour together until you have smooth dough; add water drops if necessary.

Knead dough for 10-15 minutes, until smooth, firm, and elastic.

Separate into two pieces; put to one side.

Flour your work surface.

Roll out one piece of dough, from the middle and turning occasionally; flour if necessary to keep it from sticking. To keep the dough from falling apart, once quite spread out, roll it around rolling pin, and, then, turn the rolling pin; you can, as you are unrolling the dough, gently stretch it by holding the unrolled part firm and pulling gently away with the rolling pin.

Keep on flipping and rolling until dough is very thin and transparent.

Cut ravioli squares or rectangles. With the former, put filling on one square, top with another square, and seal with egg wash. With the latter, top one end with filling, fold over, and twist together at edges, using egg wash.

Drop ravioli packets into salted, boiling water.

Cook for 3-5 minutes; it's fast because it's fresh and overcooking will make it soggy.

Rosemary Mozzarella du Pain de Blé

Ingredients:

¼ cup warm water
2¼ teaspoons (or 1 package) active dry yeast
1 cup heavy cream
1 large egg, lightly beaten
1 Tablespoon sugar
¾ teaspoon NapaStyle® gray sea salt
1 Tablespoon crushed rosemary
1 cup shredded mozzarella cheese
1 teaspoon crushed oregano
¼ teaspoon crushed garlic
4 cups sifted wheat flour (plus a bit more)

Directions:

In large bowl, mix water and yeast. Add milk, egg, sugar, NapaStyle gray sea salt, rosemary, spices and cheese. Stir. Add 3 cups flour and mix well. Add in enough flour to make a dough add enough flour to make the dough pliable and it will not stick to the bowl. Knead dough on lightly floured surface for 4 minutes, adding more flour as needed until the dough is soft and smooth to the touch. Place dough in medium greased bowl (use butter not grease). Lightly butter top. Cover with clean towel and let rise in warm, draft-free place for 1 hour or until doubled in size.

Punch down dough. Roll out dough for 4 minutes until bubbles are removed. Separate one third of the dough and set aside, make a loaf out of the other two-thirds. Place loaf in greased (butter and flour) bread pan. Take remaining dough separate into 3 sections and roll into three long strips about 2 inches longer than the bread pan. Braid. Place on top if the loaf pinching and tucking the ends to the rest of the loaf. Cover and let rise in warm, draft-free place for 45 minutes or until doubled in size.

Bake bread at 350° F for 45 minutes or until the bread it light brown or sounds hollow when the top is tapped. Remove bread from pan and let cool on rack.

Savory Toast Points

Ingredients:

Any bread (See Recipes for Bread)
Herbs blended with butter (See Recipes for Garnishes)

Directions:

Cut ½ inch slices of bread from loaf.

Trim crust off slices; save crust, by freezing, for bread pudding some other time.

Toast and lightly butter (full coverage) with savory butter.

Serve with various dips, spreads, cheeses and/or fruits. The key is in knowing which herbs match which main course (i.e. tarragon with fish; oregano with red meat; and clove with pork.

Simple Butter Croissants

This is an old Charles-family recipe, most likely passed down from Cecile's mother's side of the family. Cecile says this somewhat in jest, because she stole this and several other recipes out of her grandmothers' recipe box; not so much passed down, then, as spirited away, back when Cecile was a teenager. Cecile isn't quite sure why she chose this over a piece of glassware (her Grandma had lots of "depression glass"), or even over a piece of jewelry, except, even when she was young, Cecile knew a good thing when she saw/tasted it.

Ingredients:

1¼ teaspoons active dry yeast
3 Tablespoons warm water (110° degrees F)
3 teaspoon white sugar
1¾ cups all-purpose flour
1½ teaspoons salt
⅔ cup warm milk
2 Tablespoons olive oil
⅔ cup unsalted butter, softened
1 egg
1 Tablespoon water
2 drops of honey

Directions:

Combine yeast, warm water, and 1 teaspoon sugar; put aside until creamy and frothy.

Measure flour into mixing bowl.

Add 2 teaspoons sugar and salt dissolved in warm milk.

Add yeast mixture.

Mix.

Add oil.

Mix well.

Knead until smooth.

Cover, and let rise until three times as large.

Carefully punch down dough.

Let rise, again, until doubled.

Carefully punch down dough.

Refrigerate for 20 minutes.

Stir butter until soft and smooth; put to one side.

Pat dough into 14" x 8" rectangle.

Smear butter over top two thirds of rectangle, leaving ¼" margin all around.

Fold unbuttered third over middle third, and butter lower third.

Turn 90°, so folds are to left and right.

Roll out into a 14" x 6" rectangle.

Smear butter over top two-thirds of rectangle, leaving ¼" margin all around.

Fold unbuttered third over middle third, and butter lower third.

Sprinkle lightly with flour.

Put in a plastic bag.

Refrigerate 2 hours.

Unwrap.

Sprinkle with flour.

Carefully, punch down.

Roll to a 14" x 5" rectangle.

Smear butter over top two thirds of rectangle, leaving ¼" margin all around.

Fold unbuttered third over middle third, and butter lower third.

Turn 90°, so folds are to left and right.

Roll out into a 14" x 5" rectangle.

Smear butter over top two thirds of rectangle, leaving ¼" margin all around.

Fold unbuttered third over middle third, and butter lower third.

Fold and wrap.

Put in plastic bag.

Refrigerate for 2 hours.

Roll out dough into a 20" x 5" rectangle.

Cut in half crosswise.

Chill one-half of dough.

Roll out other half into a 15" x 5" rectangle.

Cut into three 5" x 5" squares.

Cut each square in half diagonally.

Roll each triangle lightly to elongate the point, and make it 7 inches long.

Grab the other 2 points, and stretch them out slightly as you roll it up.

Place on a baking sheet, curving dough slightly into crescent-shape.

Let rise until puffy and light.

In a small bowl, beat egg, 1 Tablespoon water, a couple drops of honey.

Glaze raised croissants lightly with egg-wash.

Bake in a preheated 475° degree oven for 12-15 minutes.

While baking, you can begin doing the same for the dough in the refrigerator.

Spicy Puff Chips

Ingredients:

Pâté à Choux, unbaked (See Recipe for Pâté à Choux)
½ teaspoon chili powder
½ teaspoon white pepper
½ teaspoon ground cumin
1 teaspoon savory salt (See Recipe for Savory Salt)
1 teaspoon full clarified butter
Red-Pepper Flakes

Directions:

Blend chili powder, white pepper, ground cumin, and savory salt; put aside until later.

Very gently roll pâté À Choux out very thinly (⅛") on baking sheets.

Bake in preheated 350° oven until brown.

Brush with clarified butter.

Sprinkle with red-pepper flakes.

Spirits of Bread Pudding

Although not officially a "bread", this is certainly a mighty tasty bread substitute. While its recipe includes a great deal more than would be found in a normal bread pudding, we've always found it a very special delight for our taste buds.

Ingredients:

5 eggs, beaten
¾ cup sugar
¼ teaspoon nutmeg
¼ teaspoon cinnamon
¼ teaspoon white pepper
1½ cups heavy cream
½ cup milk
¼ teaspoon brandy (or rum extract)
6 cups bread cubes
1 cup fresh pineapple, cubed, puréed
1 cup fresh white nectarine, cubed, puréed
1 cup fresh white peaches, cubed, puréed
1 cup brandy (or rum spirits)

Directions:

Combine eggs, sugar, nutmeg, cinnamon, pepper in 3-quart casserole.

Add heavy cream and ¼ cup milk.

Stir until thoroughly mixed; set aside for later.

Take 4 cups bread cubes and soak in remaining ¼ cup of milk until soft.

Combine soaked bread/milk and ¼ teaspoon brandy in a blender.

Pour into casserole dish.

Add remaining 2 cups bread cubes and all of the fruit.

Stir.

Let stand until bread cubes become thoroughly saturated.

Preheat oven to 350° F.

Bake in 350° preheated oven for 45 minutes, or until the top of the pudding springs back when lightly tapped.

Cool.

Brush 1 cup (yes, the whole cup) across the top of the pudding.

Serve hot or cold.

Top with one of our sweet garnishes (See Recipes for Garnishes).

Tomato Oat Bread

Ingredients:

2 cups spicy dried tomatoes
⅓ cup lukewarm water
1 cup oat bran
2 cups boiling water
2 packs active dry yeast
½ cup honey
2 Tablespoons soft butter (or nonfat butter spread)
3 cups oat flour
3 cups whole wheat flour
1 Tablespoon cinnamon
1 Tablespoon ginger
½ teaspoon paprika
½ cup apple cider
Clarified butter (See Recipe for Clarified Butter)

Directions:

Preheat oven to 325° F.

Soak tomatoes in ⅓ cup warm water until pliable (about 15 minutes); put aside until later.

In a large mixing bowl, soak oat bran in 2 cups boiling water for half an hour.

Add the yeast.

Add honey and butter.

Add out flour, wheat flour, cinnamon, ginger, and paprika, a little at a time at a time, mixing thoroughly.

Add hydrated tomatoes.

Slowly add cider to the stiff dough to help make kneading easier.

Put a towel over the bowl and let the mix rise.

Once dough has doubled in size, halve.

Split each half into 3 portions.

Shape each of 3 portions into long rolls.

Braid the three long rolls.

Put braided dough on well-oiled and floured baking pan.

Bake for 50-55 minutes.

Brush with clarified butter (See Recipe for Clarified Butter).

Bake for final 5 minutes.

Remove from oven, and cool.

World Grain Baby Breads

Ingredients:

⅓ cup stone-ground corn meal
⅓ cup old-fashioned oats
⅓ cup rye flour
⅓ cup whole-wheat flour
⅓ cup stone-ground whole wheat flour
½ cup flax seeds
½ cup hulled hemp seeds
½ cup hulled millet
½ cup whole caraway seeds
½ chia seeds
½ cup organic amaranth grain
½ cup wheat germ
2 cups boiling water
1½ packages of dry yeast
½ cup lukewarm water
1 teaspoon sugar
4½ to 5 cups unbleached bread flour
4 to 6 tbsp. honey
6 teaspoon butter
Clarified butter (See Recipe for Clarified Butter)

Directions:

Mix cornmeal, oats, rye flour, whole-wheat flour, flax seeds, hemp seeds, millet seeds, caraway seeds, chia seeds, amaranth grain, and wheat germ in a large boil.

Pour in boiling water.

Cover.

Let stand for an hour.

Dissolve yeast in ½ cup lukewarm water.

Add 1 teaspoon of sugar and stir; set aside until later.

Add dissolved yeast to bowl of ingredients.

Add bread flour, ½ cup at a time, stirring until blended.

Knead dough on a floured bread board until smooth (and it bounces back) about 12 minutes, adding as little flour as possible, to make a soft dough.

Make a nice round shape with the dough and place in a clean, oiled bowl, turning dough to coat on all sides with oil.

Cover and let rise in a warm, draft-free place until doubled in size (approximately 2 hours).

Punch down and divide into several mini loaves.

Place mini loaves in buttered and floured mini pans.

Punch thumb into each loaf, making a dent.

Let rise until double in size.

Bake at 325°F for about 1 hour.

Use toothpick to poke the loaves and come out clean.

Remove loaves from pans, and place loaves on rack for cooling.

Brush still-warm loaves with clarified butter.

NATURAL DRINKS

Apple-Onion Tea

This is very good for a cold, or flu.

Ingredients:

1 teaspoon white tea
½ cup water
2 green apples, peeled and cored
¼ small white onion
2½ cups of water
1 teaspoon lemon juice
1 teaspoon lime juice

Directions:

Put white tea in brewing spoon and steep in ½ cup of water; put aside until later.

Gently cook apples and onions in 2½ cups of water (about 20 minutes).

Strain, and add steeped tea to apples and onions.

Serve hot.

Bright Eye Juice

Ingredients:

1 cup grapefruit
1 cup kiwi fruit
1 cup carrots
½ cup water
2 drop hot sauce
4 dried dates, peeled

Directions:

In a blender, purée grapefruit, kiwi, and carrots.

Add water, hot sauce, and dates.

Blend until smooth.

Strain, saving the pulp to add to any salad green.

Carrot-Pineapple Spritz

Ingredients:

4 carrots, blanched
3 cups pineapple, peeled and cored
1 cup apple juice, fresh
¼ drop peppermint
3 cups crushed ice

Directions:

In a blender, purée carrots and pineapple.

Add apple juice, peppermint, and crushed ice.

Blend.

Serve immediately.

Dragon's Heart Smoothie

Ingredients:

¾ cup honey-flavored Greek yogurt
2 dragon fruits, quartered, skin removed
½ cup strawberries, halved
½ cup seeded and diced Roma tomatoes
½ cup seeded Bing cherries
1 teaspoon honey
Just a little lemon water
Crushed Ice

Directions:

Blend all ingredients to desired consistency.

Add lemon water to thin.

Fruited Plain

Ingredients:

1 package gelatin
1 cup meringue (See Recipe for Meringue)

1 cup sliced fresh peaches
1 cup fresh pineapple
½ cup fresh apricot
2 cups passion fruit
¼ of one mild banana pepper
1 cup heavy cream, whipped
1 cup vanilla ice cream
1½ cups filtered water
2 cups crushed ice
6 Tablespoons Grand Marnier Liqueur

Directions:

Make gelatin per package instructions.

Refrigerate.

Make meringue.

Refrigerate.

Blanch peaches, pineapple, apricot, passion fruit, and banana pepper.

Cool.

Peel and remove pits, any core, and seeds.

Purée; put to one side.

Whip cream.

Add meringue, gelatin, and ice cream.

In blender, whip until frothy.

Add water, crushed ice, and Grand Marnier.

Blend until smooth.

Mother's Dragon Milk

Ingredients:

3 peeled dragon fruit
15 Glera (Prosecco) grapes (no substitutes), peeled
½ cup heavy cream
½ teaspoon honey
½ anise seed, ground
1 cup crushed ice
⅛ teaspoon ground licorice root

Directions:

In a blender, purée dragon fruit and grapes.

Add heavy cream, honey, anise, and ice.

Blend.

Top with ground licorice root.

We can recommend this with the addition of 1 jigger of gin and ½ jigger of Benedictine.

Orange & Green Iced Tea

Actually, this is golden-brown; the seeming misnomer of its name attributed to the color of its ingredients.

Ingredients:

1 green tea bag
2 sweet oranges, quartered, peeled and seeded
A dash (1/16 teaspoon) clove, ground
A dash (1/16 teaspoon) sage, ground
A dash (1/16 teaspoon) peppermint, ground
1 drop walnut oil
I slice of orange, unpeeled

Directions:

Steep tea bag in hot water until very dark.

In blender, purée oranges until smooth.

Add steeped tea, clove, sage, peppermint, and walnut oil.

Blend.

Refrigerate

Serve over ice.

Garnish glass with a slice of unpeeled orange.

Parsley and Lime

Cecile's Grammy accompanied this recipe with the notation, "Good for headaches and pep!"

Ingredients:

7 strands of parsley
3 limes squeezed for the juice
1 cup water
1 teaspoon honey

Directions:

Blend all ingredients until drinkable.

Strain if you find the green "bits" disconcerting.

Peach-Tomato Chill

Ingredients:

½ cup fresh peaches, sautéed, puréed
½ cup fresh tomatoes, seeded, peeled
¼ teaspoon butter (for sauté)
1 cup crushed ice
1½ cup white wine
1 Tablespoon coconut shredded and chopped
¼ teaspoon almond extract

Directions:

Sauté peaches and tomatoes in ¼ teaspoon butter.

In a blender, purée sautéed peaches and tomatoes.

Add ice, wine, coconut, and almond extract, and blend.

Pomegranate Chirp

Ingredients:

¼ cup simple syrup (see Recipe for Simple Syrup)
2 cups pomegranate fruit
¼ teaspoon Mediterranean Spice (see Recipe for Mediterranean Spice)
¼ teaspoon Hawaiian Spice (see Recipe for Hawaiian Spice)
½ cup red grape juice
½ cup sweet red wine
½ cup brandy
1½ cups crushed Ice
Juice from 1 squeezed lemon

Directions:

De-seed pomegranates and put in blender.

Add all the other ingredients.

Blend well.

The Attorney

This is a home-remedy for upset stomach. Like the attorney, it's named after, it's not all that palatable, but it gets the job done.

Ingredients:

½ cup water
½ cup club soda
½ banana, puréed
1 Tablespoon lemon
1 Tablespoon lime
½ teaspoon powdered dark chocolate
1 teaspoon orange bitters
1 Tablespoon vinegar
3 Tablespoons tomato juice
½ teaspoon hot sauce

Directions:

In a blender, purée banana, lemon, and lime.

Add powdered chocolate, orange bitters, vinegar, tomato juice, and hot sauce.

Blend.

Drink quickly, with nostrils pinched between forefinger and thumb.

White Carnations

!!WARNING!!

Never use edible flowers that have been sprayed with pesticides; meaning, beware of flowers from any grocery or hardware store. It's best to grow them yourself, or buy them from a florist you can trust, like Destiny Floral (http://www.theheartofspokane.com) here, in Spokane, WA, where this book was written.

Ingredients:

1 cup white carnations (about 3 flowers)
1 white dianthus
2½ cups crushed ice
2 cups Riesling wine
⅛ teaspoon licorice extract
2 teaspoons heavy cream
6 grains of salt

Directions:

Cut carnations flowers from their bitter base and stems.

Wash and dry each petal.

Chop carnation and dianthus very finely.

Put in blender and purée with 2½ cups ice.

Add Riesling wine, licorice extract, heavy cream, and salt.

Blend until frothy.

MAIN COURSES

Blueberry Stuffed Veal Cutlets

Ingredients:

6 veal cutlets, (special cut by butcher to 10" long)
1 cup flour
½ teaspoon paprika
¼ teaspoon NapaStyle® gray sea salt
¼ teaspoon white pepper
Spritz butter
2 Tablespoon olive oil
1 clove garlic, minced
¾ cup Vegetable Stock (see Recipe for Vegetable Stock)
1 Tablespoon honey
2 eggs
1 cup blueberries, rinsed & drained
1 cup goat cheese
2 slices bread, crust removed, crumbled loosely
1 cup dry white wine
White Butter-Wine (see Recipe for White Butter-Wine)

Directions:

Rinse veal, and pat dry.

Pound veal strips thin; set aside.

Combine ⅓ cup flour, paprika, salt, and pepper.

Coat veal on both sides.

Spritz hot skillet with butter.

Add olive oil.

Add veal and sauté spice side until golden brown (or veal is almost done).

Remove veal from pan, seared side down; set aside.

To pan, add garlic, Vegetable Stock, ⅔ cup flour, honey, eggs, blueberries, cheese, bread, and wine.

Bring to boil, scraping browned bits, and stirring continuously until thoroughly blended.

Spoon mixture onto veal, and roll, seared side outward.

Place veal rolls, length-wise, side by side, in glass baking dish.

Cook in preheated 325° oven for 30 minutes, spritzing with white wine every 5 minutes.

Top with White Butter-Wine (see Recipe for White Butter-Wine).

Chopper Beef

Ingredients:

3 pounds red beef, lean, ground
1 green pepper, finely chopped

1 onion, finely chopped
1 cup black lentils
1 garlic clove, peeled, minced
1 lime, peeled, seeded, finely chopped
4 Tablespoons flour
2 eggs
1 teaspoon oregano
½ teaspoon cumin
1 cup tomatoes, skinned, seeded, puréed
½ cup vegetable stock
10 black olives, chopped
½ cup raisins
2 medium potatoes, finely diced
2 teaspoons butter
Olive oil
1 cup lime juice
1 cup dry white wine (Nodland Cellars, in Spokane offers a lovely assortment of white wines this would be the place to find that white wine.)

Directions:

In a large mixing bowl, combine all ingredients except olive oil, lime and wine.

Mix evenly.

Form into 5-inch diameter, 1-inch thick, patties.

Sauté patties, until done, in olive oil, lime, and white wine.

Lamb Patties in Cranberry-Pinot Noir Sauce

Ingredients:

2 pounds lamb, extra-lean, ground
1½ cup bread crumbs, fresh (see Recipe for Break Crumbs)
½ cup celery, finely chopped
½ cup onions, finely chopped
2 eggs
2 teaspoons garlic, minced
¼ teaspoon pepper
Cranberry Pinot Noir Sauce (see Recipe for Cranberry-Pinot Noir Sauce)

Directions:

Lightly oil a large, shallow baking dish; set aside.

In a large bowl, combine lamb, crumbs, celery, onions, eggs, garlic, and pepper.

Mix well.

Shape into 4" diameter patties.

Layer patties over bottom of baking dish.

Bake in preheated 375° oven for 20 minutes, turning contents once.

Remove from oven, and drain grease.

Transfer patties to heated chafing dish.

Top with Cranberry-Pinot Noir Sauce.

Lion's Roar

This is a vegetarian dish that may be served with a meat hors d'oeuvre, or nutty salad.

Ingredients:

4 two-ounce slices Gruyère cheese
4 Tablespoons heavy cream
2 Bottles Amontillado sherry, room temperature
4 thin slices yellow onion
8 thin slices of French bread
Clarified butter (See Recipe for Clarified Butter)
2 Tablespoons butter
4 large Lion's Mane Mushrooms
    (See http://www.alohamedicinals.com)
1 garlic clove ground
½ Tablespoon fresh squeezed lemon
1 Tablespoon lemon zest
Pepper to taste

Directions:

Melt Gruyère cheese and heavy cream.

Slowly add sherry, keep at room temperature; set aside for later.

Caramelize onions, keeping their shape; set under warmer until later.

Using cookie cutter, cut one large round from each of 4 bread slices.

Toast bread rounds and very lightly brush with clarified butter; set aside until later.

Melt one Tablespoon of butter in a skillet over medium-high heat.

Add mushrooms.

Cover pan.

Cook slightly.

Drain liquid.

Add remaining butter and garlic.

Cook until brown (don't toss but keep moving to avoid sticking).

Using 4 low-slung bowls, place one toasted round of bread in each bowl.

Pour equal amounts of cheese into each bowl.

Cut remaining 4 slices of bread to curve just inside the bowls with tips in the cheese.

Place one onion in center of each bowl.

Top each onion with one mushroom.

Brush with clarified butter.

Sprinkle with zest.

Serve immediately, and spritz a little sherry onto each, followed by a grind (or grinds) of pepper.

Orange Almond Chicken

Ingredients:

4 large chicken breasts, boneless, skinless
4 Tablespoons flour
½ teaspoon NapaStyle® gray sea salt
½ teaspoon black pepper
1 egg, beaten
1 cup almonds, sliced
1 Tablespoon honey
Butter enough to cover pan
2 oranges, peeled, thinly sliced
1 cup orange juice
4 Tablespoons orange liqueur
1 Tablespoon brown sugar
1 Tablespoon Roux (see Recipe for Roux)
½ teaspoon Arabian Spice (see Recipe for Arabian Spice)

Directions:

Coat chicken with flour.

Sprinkle with salt and black pepper.

Dip one side of each floured chicken breast into egg.

Dip same side of each into almonds.

Place in large buttered pan, on medium-high heat, almond side down.

Cook for 3-5 minutes (or until almonds toast).

Turn chicken breasts.

Turn heat to medium-low.

Cook for 10-12 minutes (or until chicken is no longer pink in center).

Place in a baking dish.

Drizzle with honey.

Cover with orange slices.

Pour orange juice into bottom of the baking dish.

Broil for 10 minutes.

Quickly, remove chicken; set aside in warming bag.

Remove orange slices from baking dish; set aside on plate.

With rubber spatula, stir into baking dish 4 Tablespoons orange liqueur, brown sugar, Roux, and Arabian Spice.

Stir until syrup; set aside.

On serving plates, put orange slices.

Place chicken on orange slices.

Drizzle all with syrup enough to provide small pool.

Ostrich and Tortellini

Ingredients:

Tortellini dough (See Recipe for Tortellini Dough)
3 cups fresh Parmesan cheese tortellini
1 cup Parmesan cheese, grated
1 large red onion, loosely chopped
2 cloves garlic, minced
1 red pepper. diced
1 lb. ground ostrich meat
1½ cup fresh mushrooms
5 cups vegetable broth (see Recipe for Vegetable Broth)
½ cup picante (see Recipe for Picante)
1 teaspoon crushed basil
1½ cups stewed tomatoes (fresh)
10 dried apricots, cubed

Directions:

Make enough tortellini dough for this recipe.

Fill small squares of dough with fresh Parmesan cheese, saving some cheese for later sprinkling.

Fold and shape tortellini to your preference; usually fold like a diaper, and, then connected at the ends; put to one until later

Sauté onion, garlic, red pepper, ostrich, and mushrooms in pan; put to one side until later.

In a large pot, stir broth, picante, and basil.

Bring to a boil.

Add stuffed tortellini and simmer, uncovered, 10 to 20 minutes (or until soft).

Stir in sautéed mixture, as well as stewed tomatoes and apricots.

Sprinkle on grated Parmesan cheese before serving.

Peperoni Verdi Gamberoni Farciti
(Green Peppers Stuffed With Shrimp)

This dish provides a strongly pungent aroma while cooking; you might want to open a window or door to the outside.

Ingredients:

4 large green peppers, whole
8 slices mozzarella cheese
4 cups pulled spinach, washed, chopped loosely
1 pound baby shrimp
½ cup grated Parmesan cheese
1 teaspoon black pepper
1 Tablespoon Italian Spice (see Recipe for Italian Spice)
4 cloves garlic, minced
4 Tablespoons clarified butter (See Recipe for Clarified Butter)
1 cup fresh lemon juice
½ cup Tawny Port

Directions:

Blanch peppers in big pan of boiling water.

Cool, peel, and de-seed.

Spritz inside each pepper with butter, lemon juice, and port.

Place in 9-inch square glass baking dish.

Stuff each pepper, in the following sequence: mozzarella, spinach, shrimp, Parmesan cheese, pepper, Italian Spice, minced garlic...then repeat the stuffing sequence.

Spritz outside each pepper with butter, lemon, and port.

Cook in a 350° oven about an hour.

Serve hot and topped with Shrimp Cream (See Recipe for Shrimp Cream).

Pork 'n' Pine

Ingredients:

4 pork medallions
1 teaspoon extra-virgin olive oil
1 teaspoon butter
2 cups sun dried tomatoes (See Recipe for Dried Tomatoes)
1½ Tablespoons pine nuts, toasted, finely chopped
2 Tablespoons fresh lemon juice
½ cup lemon zest
1 teaspoon fresh oregano, chopped
½ teaspoon Allspice
1 teaspoon Cajun Spice (See Recipe for Cajun Spice)
1 teaspoon parsley, chopped
1 garlic clove, peeled, crushed
Salt
Black pepper, freshly ground
Water spritzer

Directions:

Sear the pork medallions in a sauté pan, using ½-teaspoon olive oil, and ½-teaspoon butter; set aside, leaving in sauté pan, until later.

In an iron skillet, over medium heat, add tomatoes, pine nuts, lemon juice, zest, oregano, Allspice, Cajun Spice, parsley, garlic, ½-teaspoon butter, ½-teaspoon olive oil, salt, and pepper.

Stir until everything is toasted; set aside until later.

Pre-heat broiler.

Pour tomato/nut mixture over pork medallions, and cover with foil lid.

Place in broiler for 10-15 minutes.

Carefully, remove from broiler, partially peel back foil lid, and spritz contents.

Quickly recover with foil and steam for 3 minutes.

Remove foil.

Spoon tomato/nut mixture onto each plate and top with pork medallion.

Salmon Stir

Ingredients:

1 pound red potatoes, 1-inch pieces
1 Tablespoon Oriental Spice (see Recipe for Oriental Spice)

2 Tablespoons clarified butter (see Recipe for Clarified Butter)
2 teaspoons olive oil
¼ teaspoon mustard seed, ground
¼ teaspoon white pepper, freshly ground
1 Tablespoon balsamic vinegar
4 Tablespoons sherry
8 ounces fresh salmon, cubed
2 cups Enokitake mushrooms, cubed
1 cup zucchini, cubed
1 large avocado, pitted, peeled, cubed
1 cup Bing cherries, pitted, quartered

Directions:

Put potatoes in a bowl and toss them with ½-Tablespoon Oriental Spice, 1-Tablespoon clarified butter, and 1-teaspoon olive oil.

Put potatoes on a flat cooking pan.

Roast in oven until potatoes are brown.

In the meantime, whisk vinegar, dry mustard, white pepper, ½-Tablespoon Oriental Spice, balsamic vinegar, wine, 1-teaspoon olive oil, and 1-Tablespoon clarified butter; put to one side.

Place salmon, mushrooms, zucchini, avocado, and cherries in a sauté pan.

Cover with whisked ingredients and sauté until golden and/or nicely crusted.

Place sautéed ingredients in an elongated glass baking dish and cook in 350° oven for 10 minutes.

Serve immediately.

Sea Bass and White Sauce

Ingredients:

6 sea bass, fillets
½ cup butter
1 Tablespoon Mediterranean Spice (see Recipe for Mediterranean Spice)
1 cup dry white wine
1½ cups White Sauce (see Recipe for White Sauce)
2 cups hearts of palm
Lemon slices

Directions:

Pat fillets dry with paper towels.

In baking dish, melt butter.

Dip fish in butter, and place in frying pan, skin side down.

Sprinkle Mediterranean Spice.

Pour wine over fish.

Bake in preheated 350° oven 10 minutes, basting frequently with pan juices.

Ladle 1 cup White Sauce onto a serving platter.

Layer on hearts of palm.

Layer on fish.

Ladle on rest of sauce, and garnish with lemon slices.

Tiger Shrimp & Blackberries on Black Rice

Try to time the cooking of your rice and shrimp so that they're ready at one and the same time.

Ingredients:

Rice
2 Tablespoons Cajun Spice (see Cajun Spice)
30 large tiger shrimp, peeled, deveined
¼ cup melted butter
2 Tablespoons fresh lemon juice
3 cups blackberries
1 bay leaf
2 teaspoons black pepper
2 Tablespoons fresh garlic, minced
2 teaspoons hot sauce
1 Tablespoon honey
1 cup dry white wine

Directions:

Cook rice per directions on package.

Add ½ Tablespoon Cajun Spice.

Separately, combine uncooked shrimp with remaining ingredients.

Place in buttered shallow baking dish, and toss to coat.

Sauté, stirring occasionally, for about 15 minutes (or until shrimp are pink and completely cooked).

Spoon over rice.

Venison Medallions

Ingredients:

1 cup water
½ cup red wine
⅛ teaspoon NapaStyle® gray sea salt
⅛ teaspoon black pepper
4 teaspoons beef bouillon, granules
1 teaspoon dried onion, ground
2 pounds venison, 3-inch squares
2 cups yellow onions, diced

Directions:

In a sauté pan, place water, wine, salt, pepper, bouillon, and dried onion.

Add venison and diced onions.

Cover with tight lid.

Cook on low heat for 120-180 minutes.

Make sure juice remains in the pan, throughout; add more water, during cooking, if necessary.

CASSEROLES

Beer Venison Casserole

There's no binder (cheese, flour, etc.) to "hold" this together; so, it's best served in 4-inch tall square heat-resistant glass serving dishes.

Ingredients:

4 carrots, thinly sliced
4 celery stalks, chopped
2 cups beer, preferably dark stout
1 small onion, finely chopped
¼ teaspoon NapaStyle® gray sea salt
¼ teaspoon white pepper
1½ pounds venison, ⅛" x 2" strips
1½ cup Rainier cherries, pitted, chopped
1 cup blackberries
1 teaspoon fresh thyme, chopped
½ teaspoon cayenne pepper
5 medium sweet potatoes, thinly sliced
Mediterranean Spice (see Recipe for Mediterranean Spice)
Butterfly Butter (see Recipe for Butterfly Butter)

Directions:

Blanch carrots, and celery in ½ cup beer; set aside.

In sauté pan, caramelize onion in sea salt and pepper.

Place venison strips on onion.

Add ½ cup beer, cherries, and blackberries.

Add thyme and cayenne pepper.

Simmer until venison is soft and done; set aside.

Pour 1 cup beer into glass casserole baking dish.

On beer, begin layering sweet potato slices, carrots and celery, onion, cherries, and venison (seasoning with Mediterranean Spice as you do).

Continuing layering until you end up with last of carrots and celery.

Tent tin foil over baking dish.

Bake in preheated 250° oven 30 minutes (using baster to move liquid from bottom to top at five-minute intervals).

Remove from oven.

Cut straight down into casserole and gently plate pieces to show layering.

Baste with excess juice.

Serve with Butterfly Butter.

Black Rice & Minced Meat Casserole

Ingredients:

1½ cups black rice
2½ cups water, boiling
1½ pounds lean beef, ¼" cubes
1 teaspoon Savory Spice (see Recipe for Savory Spice)
1 teaspoon sage, ground
2 cups raisins, quartered
½ cup sugar, moist
½ cup citron, diced
½ cup candied lemon peel, cubed
½ cup candied orange peel, cubed
1 Tablespoon nutmeg
¼ cup walnuts, ground
¼ cup almonds, ground
¼ cup pecans, ground
1 cup apples, peeled, diced
2 Tablespoons lemon zest
2 Tablespoons butter
1½ packets clear gelatin
1 cup brandy

Directions:

Combine rice and boiling water.

Cook rice until done; set aside.

In a large mixing bowl, thoroughly blend all other ingredients; set aside.

In a large baking mold, press in the rice, leaving hollow for fruit and meat mixture.

Ladle fruit and meat mixture into hollow, and tightly pack.

Chill overnight.

Place in preheated 275° oven for 45 minutes.

Unmold and serve.

Chicken Casserole Topped With Wine Sauce

Ingredients:

1½ cups brown rice
¼ cup butter
2 cups truffle mushrooms, chopped
1 large onion, chopped
1 clove garlic, minced
6 chicken breasts, cut in short strips
2 cups dry white wine
2 Tablespoons flour
1 teaspoon thyme, fresh, minced
1 teaspoon Arabian Spice (see Recipe for Arabian Spice)
½ teaspoon NapaStyle® gray sea salt
½ teaspoon pepper
2 Tablespoons parsley, fresh, minced

Directions:

Cook rice as directed on package.

Pack cooked rice into bottom of glass casserole dish; set aside.

In a sauté pan, use some butter to sauté mushrooms, onion, and garlic; set aside.

In a sauté pan, use some butter to sear/brown chicken strips; set aside.

In a blender, combine remaining butter with wine, flour, thyme, Arabian Spice, salt, and pepper; set aside.

Layer chicken on top of the rice.

Layer sautéed mushroom, onion, and garlic mix atop chicken.

Sprinkle on parsley.

Cook in preheated 350° oven, for about 20 minutes.

Top with blended mixture.

Chicken Cordon-Bleu Casserole

Ingredients:

Pie Dough (see Recipe for Pie Dough)
6 chicken breasts, skinless, boneless, ¼-inch cubes
2 cups mozzarella cheese, shredded
2 cups Swiss cheese, shredded
¼ teaspoon NapaStyle® gray sea salt
¼ teaspoon oregano
1 Tablespoon onion, shaved
1 Tablespoon garlic clove, shaved
⅛ teaspoon black pepper, ground
Mediterranean Spice (see Recipe for Mediterranean Spice)
Butter
Parmesan cheese

Directions:

Prepare Pie Dough for top and bottom of 14" x 18" glass baking dish.

Place one layer of dough on the bottom of baking dish.

Bake in preheated 350° oven for 10 minutes (or until crust is lightly brown).

Remove from oven; set aside.

Turn oven to 450°.

Fill baking dish with consecutive layers of chicken, mozzarella cheese, Swiss cheese, seasoned with salt, oregano, shaved onion, garlic, pepper, and Mediterranean Spice, to taste, until dish is full.

Bake 30 minutes.

Remove and cover with pie dough.

Return to oven.

Bake 15 minutes (or until top is lightly brown).

Remove from oven.

Brush on butter.

Grate on Parmesan cheese.

Serve hot.

Corn Fritters and Spicy Pork Casserole

Ingredients:

2 cups vegetable oil
1 cup cream corn
1 egg
1 cup all-purpose flour
¾ teaspoon baking powder
½ teaspoon salt
1 teaspoon sugar
1 Tablespoon medium-dry sherry +1 cup medium-dry sherry, in spritzer
1 Tablespoon cornstarch
3 Tablespoons soy sauce
2 teaspoons Asian sesame oil
1 pound pork loin, boneless, thinly sliced into 2" x ¼" strips
3 Tablespoons olive oil
2 teaspoons ginger, fresh, minced, peeled
2 teaspoons garlic, minced
½ teaspoon hot red-pepper flakes, dried (See Recipe for Red-pepper flakes)
1 Tablespoon Hawaiian Spice (see Recipe for Hawaiian Spice)
1 large red bell pepper, ¼" strips
1 cup cashews, salted, roasted, crushed

Directions:

In a deep fryer, heat oil to 350°.

In a small bowl, mix cream corn and egg; set aside.

In a medium bowl, mix flour, baking powder, salt, and sugar.

Add corn and egg mixture.

Mix.

Drop batter, ⅛ cup at a time, into the hot oil.

Deep-fry until golden brown, turning once if batter doesn't turn by itself.

Remove from deep fryer and drain on paper towels; set aside.

In a bowl, combine 1 Tablespoon sherry, 1 Tablespoon cornstarch, and 1 Tablespoon soy sauce.

Stir in sesame oil.

Add pork, turning to coat well; set aside for at least 10 minutes.

Heat a large nonstick skillet over high heat until bead of water, dropped on cooking surface, sizzles into oblivion.

Add 1½ Tablespoons olive oil, and swirl pan to coat evenly.

Stir-fry 2 Tablespoons soy sauce, 1 teaspoon ginger, 1 teaspoon garlic, ¼ teaspoon pepper flakes, and 1 Tablespoon Hawaiian Spice until fragrant (about 5 seconds).

Add bell pepper, and stir-fry 2 minutes.

Add cashews, and stir-fry 2 minutes.

Transfer to bowl; set aside.

Heat remaining 1½ Tablespoons olive oil in pan until it just begins to smoke.

Stir-fry remaining ginger, garlic, and pepper flakes, until fragrant (about 5 seconds).

Add pork and stir-fry, separating strips, until browned and barely cooked (about 2 to 3 minutes).

Add green pepper and nut mixture.

Stir-fry until heated through (about 1 minute); set aside.

In a large casserole dish, stack alternating layers of pork and fritters, spritzing each layer with sherry.

Serve hot.

Fatted Lamb Blast Pasta Casserole

Ingredients:

24 ounces lamb, cubed
Clarified Butter (see Recipe for Clarified Butter)
¼ pound mushrooms, fresh, chopped
1 cup red onions, chopped
½ cup white wine
16 ounces cottage cheese
8 ounces cream cheese
8 ounces sour cream
8 ounces Greek-honey flavored yogurt
5 eggs
1 large lemon, peeled, finely chopped
Noodles, cooked, strained
½ cup cranberries, dried
Feta cheese, fresh

Directions:

Preheat oven to 350°.

In a pan, brown lamb in Clarified Butter.

Add mushrooms.

Cook until mushrooms are soft; set aside.

In a pan, brown onions in Clarified Butter.

Add all but 1 Tablespoon white wine; set aside.

In a blender, purée lamb and mushrooms, onions, cottage cheese, cream cheese, sour cream, yogurt, eggs and lemon.

Put in a lightly greased casserole dish.

Add noodles, cranberries, and 1 Tablespoon of white wine.

Toss.

Cook for 40 minutes.

Remove from oven.

Grate on feta cheese.

Return to oven until cheese is brown and casserole bubbles.

Hot Curried Fruit and Bear Meat Casserole

This is best made a day ahead of time, then reheated at 350° for ½ hour.

Ingredients:

1½ pound bear meat, cubed
1 Tablespoon Savory Spice (see Recipe for Savory Spice)
1 cup fresh pears, chopped
1 cup fresh peaches, chopped
1 cup fresh apricots, chopped
1 cup fresh pineapple chunks
¼ cup brown sugar
¼ cup butter, melted
¾ teaspoon curry powder
1 Tablespoon Roux (see Recipe for Roux)
⅛ teaspoon (more if you prefer) cinnamon
⅛ teaspoon (more if you prefer) cloves, ground

Directions:

Boil bear meat with Savory Spice for one hour.

Preheat oven to 350°.

In ungreased 9" x 13" glass baking dish, combine boiled meat with remaining ingredients, making sure the Roux is completely dissolved.

Bake for 1 hour.

Las Espinacas y Alcachofas à la Cazuela

Ingredients:

2 cups cream cheese, soft
6 Tablespoons cream
4 Tablespoons olive oil
2 teaspoons Mexican Spice (see Recipe for Mexican Spice)
1½ cups Vegetable Stock (see Recipe for Vegetable Stock)
2 cups artichoke hearts, drained, chopped
3 cup Mexican rice (see Recipe for Mexican Rice)
2 cups white corn (cut from the cob), fresh, blanched
6 cups spinach, stemmed, washed, chopped
9 one-eighth-inch slices Muenster cheese, fresh

Directions:

Blend cream cheese, cream, olive oil, Mexican Spice, and Vegetable Stock; set aside.

Place artichokes on bottom of large casserole dish.

Add layer Mexican Rice.

Add layer of corn.

Add another layer of Mexican Rice.

Add layer of spinach.

Add layer of cheese, cream, olive oil, Mexican Spice, and Vegetable Stock mixture.

Add layer of Munster cheese.

Continue layering, ending with Muenster cheese on top.

Bake, uncovered, in preheated 375° oven for 40 minutes (or until cheese is melted).

Over the Rainbow Casserole

Ingredients:

Pâté à Choux (See Recipe for Pâté à Choux Puff Pastry),
6 ten-inch trout, scaled, filleted, de-boned
Butter
½ cup water
1 teaspoon NapaStyle® gray sea salt
1 teaspoon tarragon
½ teaspoon white pepper
1½ cup bleu cheese, crumbled
½ bunch Italian parsley, finely chopped
2 lemons, peeled, de-seeded, thinly sliced
2 cups blueberries
4 pieces ripe watermelon, seedless, peeled, ½-inch strips
8 slices fresh pineapple, ½-inch strips

Directions:

Make ¼ recipe for Pâté à Choux Puff Pastry.

Refrigerate.

In hot sauté pan, sear both sides of trout, in a little butter, until brown.

Line up trout in bottom of deep casserole dish; set aside.

Whip water, salt, tarragon, and pepper.

Pour over fish in casserole dish.

Sprinkle bleu cheese evenly over fish.

Sprinkle parsley over the cheese.

Place lemon slices over parsley.

Place blueberries over lemon slices.

Place watermelon strips over blueberries.

Place pineapple strips over watermelon.

Place in preheated 300° oven for 30 minutes (or until hot, through and through).

Remove from oven; set aside.

Roll out puff pastry and place over top of casserole.

Seal the edges of pastry to casserole dish.

With a toothpick, poke holes in the pastry.

On top of pastry, write "RAINBOW" with toothpick.

Return casserole to oven.

Bake until pastry is golden brown.

Pineapple Picante Beef Casserole

This recipe is spicy hot, so beware!

Ingredients:

2 cups mandarin oranges, puréed
2 whole fresh pineapples, chopped, peeled, cored
½ cup sweet red pepper
⅓ cup Picante
3 pounds beef steak, trimmed of fat, thinly sliced across grain
Mexican Spice (see Recipe for Mexican Spice)
2 Tablespoons olive oil
1 cup shredded Mozzarella Cheese

Directions:

In medium sauce pan, gently mix oranges, ½ chopped pineapple, sweet red pepper, and Picante.

Cook on low for 10 minutes; set aside.

Sprinkle both sides of steak with Mexican Spice.

In large skillet, over medium-high heat, cook and turn steak in hot oil for 2-3 minutes (or until done).

Remove from skillet and place in glass casserole dish.

Top with rest of chopped pineapple and Picante mixture.

Cook in preheated 350° oven for 20 minutes.

Add cheese, and cook until cheese is melted.

Spinach and Capers Casserole

Ingredients:

6 cups spinach, raw
½ cup capers
1½ cups asparagus, finely chopped
1½ cups squash, finely chopped
1½ cups grapes, white, seedless, chopped
2½ cups cottage cheese
⅓ cup butter
3 eggs, beaten
¼ cup flour
½ teaspoon NapaStyle® gray sea salt
¼ teaspoon white pepper
1 teaspoon Mediterranean Spice (see Recipe for Mediterranean Spice)
White Sauce (see Recipe for White Sauce)

Directions:

In a large bowl, mix all ingredients, except White Sauce.

Spoon into large slightly greased and floured glass baking dish.

Cover with aluminum foil (or lid).

Cook in a preheated 350° oven for 150 minutes (or until done).

Top with White Sauce.

Wild Rice with Dove Casserole

Ingredients:

10 dove breasts, skinned, quartered
½ cup lime juice, freshly squeezed
½ teaspoon NapaStyle® gray sea salt
½ teaspoon white pepper
1 cup wild rice, rinsed
2 cups water
1 pound Chanterelles mushrooms
4 scallions
2 stalks celery
3 teaspoons butter
¼ teaspoon tarragon
½ cup dry white wine
1½ cup Vegetable Stock (see Recipe for Vegetable Stock)
1 cup Parmesan, fresh

Directions:

Rub dove breasts with lime juice.

Season with salt and pepper.

Refrigerate at least 12 hours, turning occasionally.

In small sauce pan, add rice and water.

Partially cook for 12 minutes.

Drain; set aside.

Chop mushrooms, scallions and celery.

Using a sauté pan, sauté in butter.

Transfer rice to bottom of glass casserole dish.

Transfer dove breasts to rice, making sure meat is evenly distributed.

Pour mushroom, scallion, and celery mixture over dove.

Add tarragon, white wine, and Vegetable Stock.

Cover and cook in preheated 325° oven for 90-105 minutes.

Remove from oven.

Grate on Parmesan just before serving hot.

STEWS

Bear Stew

Ingredients:

¼ cup flour
2 Tablespoon Italian Spice (see Recipe for Italian Spice)
2 Tablespoons Savory Spice (see Recipe for Savory Spice)
4 pounds bear meat, cubed
2 Tablespoons vegetable oil
4 Tablespoons butter
2 cups water + 2-3 quarts water
1 cup dry red wine
2 cups Vegetable Stock (see Recipe for Vegetable Stock)
1 large onion, diced
2 pounds potatoes, cubed
1 pound fresh button mushrooms, small
5 carrots, diced
1 turnip, cubed
5 parsnips, cubed
4 bay leaves

Directions:

In a plastic bag, put flour, 1 Tablespoon Italian Spice, and 1 Tablespoon Savory Spice.

Add bear meat.

Shake until meat is coated with flour and spices; set aside.

In skillet, heat oil and butter.

Add meat and brown.

Drain off grease; set aside.

In a pressure cooker, put bear meat, 2 cups water, 1 Tablespoon Italian Spice, 1 Tablespoon Savory Spice.

Cook until meat falls apart when picked up with a fork (about 60 minutes).

Transfer meat to large Dutch oven.

Pour in 2-3 quarts water, wine, and Vegetable Stock.

Add onion, potatoes, mushrooms, carrots, turnips, parsnips, and bay leaves.

In preheated 325° oven, put Dutch oven 2-3 hours, checking every 30 minutes, and adding water if necessary.

Remove bay leaves before serving.

Beef and Red Wine Stew

Ingredients:

4 Tablespoons virgin olive oil
2 pounds beef tenderloin, cubed
4 cups tomatoes, stewed, de-seeded, chopped

2 cups raw carrots, chopped
½ orange, peeled, de-seeded, puréed
4 cloves garlic, large, crushed
6 sprigs thyme, fresh, chopped
1 bay leaf
12 ounces dry red wine.
2 pints Vegetable Stock (see Recipe for Vegetable Stock)
NapaStyle® gray sea salt
Pepper

Directions:

In a spacious heavy sauté pan with well-fitting lid, add oil, and sauté beef until thoroughly cooked.

Add tomatoes, carrots, orange, garlic, thyme, and bay leaf.

Cover pan.

Simmer 15 minutes.

Add the wine.

Boil vigorously until liquid reduces by half.

Add Vegetable Stock.

Simmer, partially covered, 25 minutes.

Salt and pepper to taste

Remove bay leaf before serving.

Cantaloupe Stew

Ingredients:

½ cup cream
½ cup water
1 cup red potatoes, cooked, diced
1 cup carrots, boiled, diced
1 cup pineapple, fresh, diced
3 cups cantaloupe, peeled, diced
⅓ cup dry sherry
¼ teaspoon thyme
¼ teaspoon marjoram
⅛ teaspoon NapaStyle® gray sea salt
¼ teaspoon nutmeg
Lime slices

Directions

In a blender, purée cream, water, potatoes, carrots, pineapple, and cantaloupe to a smooth consistency.

Stir in sherry, thyme, marjoram, and salt.

Serve chilled.

Garnish with a sprinkle of nutmeg and/or lime slices.

Coconut & Corn Stew

Ingredients:

2 cups water
2 cups Vegetable Stock (see Recipe for Vegetable Stock)
1 cup onion, diced

1 cup brown basmati rice, cooked
1 cup celery, diced
3 medium cloves garlic, peeled, ground
1 Tablespoon fresh ginger, grated
¾ teaspoon coriander seeds, ground
¼ teaspoon NapaStyle® gray sea salt
¼ teaspoon red-pepper flakes, crushed
4 cups fresh corn, off of the cob, cooked
1½ cups white grapes, chopped
1½ Tablespoons coconut, raw, grated
1 cup yellow bell pepper, diced
1 cup coconut milk, unsweetened
1 teaspoon Oriental Spice (see Recipe for Oriental Spice)
2 teaspoons lime zest
3 Tablespoons lime juice, freshly squeezed
½ cup fresh cilantro, chopped

Directions:

In a large pot, over medium heat, put in water and Vegetable Stock.

Add onion, rice, celery, garlic, ginger, coriander, salt, and red-pepper flakes.

Cook for 10 minutes.

Add corn, grapes, coconut, and bell pepper.

Cover with lid.

Increase heat to high.

Bring to a boil.

Add coconut milk.

Reduce heat to medium-low.

Cover with lid.

Cook for 10 minutes.

Add Oriental Spice.

Cover with lid.

Cook for 5-6 minutes.

Add lime zest and juice.

Add cilantro.

Stir.

"Creamed" PID Stew

This recipe got its name because one of Cecile's old boyfriends arrived two hours late for a meal she'd prepared, one night, his excuse as lame as they come. Cecile, in a piqué, stuffed everything she'd prepared into a blender, and blended until it was smooth. She filled a very tall and hefty beer mug full of the preparation and brought it to him. Without a word, he slowly drank it all down, handed back the empty mug, smacked his lips, and asked for seconds. Go figure!

Ingredients:

1 pound steak, de-fatted, chopped and sautéed.
2 cups green beans, chopped and cooked
2 potatoes, baked, peeled, and chopped
2 eggs, boiled, and chopped

1 cup corn, cooked
2 tomatoes, peeled, de-seeded, chopped
2 cucumbers, peeled, de-seeded, chopped
1 cup black olives, de-seeded, chopped
1 small onion, chopped
¼ clove garlic, diced
1 cup butter lettuce, washed
1 cup red cabbage, washed
1 teaspoon A-1® Steak Sauce
2 teaspoons butter, melted
1 cup pistachio nuts, ground
2 slices French bread w/crust, crumbled
1 cup blueberries
4 ounces dry white wine
1½ cup water
1 cup heavy cream
1 Tablespoon flour
½ teaspoon sugar
¼ teaspoon oregano
⅛ teaspoon NapaStyle® gray sea salt
⅛ teaspoon pepper

Directions:

Purée ALL ingredients.

Pour into a large stew pot.

Bring to a simmer (DO NOT BOIL).

Add a little water if too thick; add more cream if too thin.

Dove & Caps Stew

Ingredients:

2 Tablespoons butter
1 cup Shiitake mushrooms, loosely chopped
1 cup Morel mushrooms, loosely chopped
1 cup Portobello mushrooms, loosely chopped
1 cup Oyster mushrooms, loosely chopped
1 large onion, chopped
14 dove breasts; cleaned, quartered
3 teaspoons water
3 cups Vegetable Stock (see Recipe for Vegetable Stock)
¼ teaspoon NapaStyle® gray sea salt
¼ teaspoon white pepper
¼ teaspoon cayenne pepper
1½ heavy cream

Directions

In a sauté pan, add 1 Tablespoon butter, and sauté loosely-chopped mushrooms (Shiitake, Morel, Portobello, and Oyster), and set aside.

In a sauté pan, caramelize onion, and set aside.

In spacious heavy sauté pan, add 1 Tablespoon butter, and brown dove breasts.

Add 3 teaspoons of water, cover, and let steam.

Add Vegetable Stock, salt, white pepper, and cayenne pepper.

Simmer (DO NOT BOIL) 1 hour (or until tender).

Add sautéed mushrooms.

Add caramelized onion.

Stew 10 minutes.

Add cream, and stir to dissolve.

Green Chili Stew

Ingredients:

2 cups black beans
1 pound extra-lean pork, boneless, cubed
1 Tablespoon butter
3½ cups Vegetable Stock (see Recipe for Vegetable Stock)
2 cups cabbage, chopped
1 bunch asparagus, chopped
1 cup white radish, chopped
4 white potatoes, washed
1 cup green chilies, medium-hot, diced
2 cloves garlic, peeled, minced
1 teaspoon green hot sauce
6 green tomatoes, peeled, de-seeded, chopped
1 Tablespoon whiskey

Directions

Soak beans overnight, rinsing twice before morning.

In sauté pan, put pork and butter.

Sear pork, browning each side; set aside.

In a big stew pot, put meat, Vegetable Stock, cabbage, asparagus, radish, potatoes, chilies, garlic, and green hot sauce.

Bring to boil.

Turn down heat.

Simmer vegetables until tender (about 60 minutes).

Add tomatoes and whiskey.

Simmer 30 minutes.

Lobster Cream Stew

Ingredients:

1 onion, finely chopped
1 stalk celery, finely chopped
1 carrot, finely chopped
6 Tablespoon butter
2½ cups lobster meat, bite-size pieces
1 bay leaf
4½ cups heavy cream
1½ cups Vegetable Stock (see Recipe for Vegetable Stock)
6 Tablespoons all-purpose flour
1 pinch celery salt
2 rose hips, ground
1 teaspoon fresh parsley, finely chopped
½ cup walnuts, finely chopped
½ cup apple, peeled, finely chopped
½ cup sherry
¼ cup brandy
¼ teaspoon lemon extract
Salt
Pepper

Directions:

In roasting pan, put onion, celery, and carrot.

Cover with water.

Put on lid.

Place in preheated 400° oven for 45 minutes.

Add butter, lobster, and bay leaf.

Add, very slowly, cream, Vegetable Stock, and flour.

Add celery salt, rose hips, parsley, walnuts, and apple.

Cook for about 20 minutes over medium heat.

Add sherry, brandy, and lemon extract.

Salt and pepper to taste.

Remove bay leaf before serving.

Nutty Vegetable Stew

Ingredients:

½ cup cashews, finely chopped
½ cup walnuts, finely chopped
½ cup sunflower seeds, finely chopped
2 Tablespoons olive oil
2 onions, large, finely chopped
4 cloves, large, peeled, minced
8 cups of water

2 Tablespoons vegetable-stock paste
4 carrots, large, chopped
1 cup broccoli, chopped
1 cup cabbage, chopped
1 cup corn
1 cup garbanzo beans
1 cup black beans
1 cup black-eyes peas
6 tomatoes, cubed
⅔ cup brown rice, uncooked
¼ teaspoon white pepper
2 cups red potatoes, peeled, cubed
¼ teaspoon oregano
⅓ cup pearl barley
¼ teaspoon chili powder
¼ teaspoon onion powder
1 cup white wine

Directions:

Purée nuts and seeds to a crunchy "butter" in blender; set aside.

Heat oil in a large pan.

Add onions, and sauté until lightly browned and tender.

Stir in garlic, being careful it doesn't burn; set aside.

Boil water.

Stir in vegetable-stock paste.

Add seed/nut butter, onion/garlic, and all remaining ingredients.

Simmer on a low heat for at least 120 minutes.

Poor Man's Saffron Stew

You have to make this in the early summer after the marigolds have bloomed.

Never use edible flowers that have been sprayed with pesticides; meaning, beware of flowers from any grocery or hardware store. It's best to grow them yourself, or buy them from a florist you can trust, like Destiny Floral... http://experiencespokane.com/destinyfloralprettythings/

...here, in Spokane, WA, where this book was written.

Ingredients:

Garlic Butter (see Recipe for Garlic Butter)
1 or 2 onions, chopped.
1 pound ground beef (very, very lean)
4-6 potatoes, peeled, diced.
2 cups rutabaga, cubed
2 cups white radish, cubed
2-ounce glass red wine
2-4 cups milk
⅓ cup marigold petals, finely chopped
Salt and black pepper to taste
1 teaspoon turmeric

Directions

In a sauté pan, sauté onion(s) in Garlic Butter, and set aside.

In a large skillet, over medium heat, brown ground beef and drain.

Remove meat from skillet and rinse to remove oils; set aside.

In large saucepan, on high, bring potatoes, rutabaga, and radish, to a slight boil.

Reduce heat to medium.

Add wine.

Cook until everything just tender (about 15 minutes).

Pour off half of the liquid.

Add browned ground beef, milk, onions, and all but a few marigold petals.

Simmer until ready to serve.

Flavor to taste with salt, pepper, and turmeric.

Sprinkle each serving with remaining marigold petals.

Rhubarb Stew

Ingredients:

2 cups red potatoes, peeled, chopped
1 cup white corn
1 cup arugula, chopped
1 cup turnips, chopped
1 cup watercress, chopped
1 cup yellow bell pepper
1 cup shiitake Mushrooms, chopped
4 stalks rhubarb, strings removed, chopped
4 stalks celery, strings removed, chopped
1 cup lentils, well-washed, drained
1 cup leeks, chopped

2 Tablespoons ginger, minced
1 Tablespoon garlic clove, fresh, minced
1 teaspoon cardamom
1 Tablespoon mustard seeds
1 Tablespoons flax seeds
3 Tablespoon sesame seeds
1 Tablespoon poppy seeds
3 Tablespoon sunflower seeds, raw
1 teaspoon clove, ground
1 teaspoon white pepper
1 chili, mild, dried, ground
NapaStyle® gray sea salt
Cilantro leaves (to taste), chopped
2 cups tomatoes, re-boiled for 10 minutes, peeled, diced

Directions

In a sauce pan, combine all ingredients, except tomatoes.

Add water to cover by 1 inch.

Cook at steady simmer until lentils and rhubarb are quite soft (20-30 minutes).

Add tomatoes.

Cook 5 minutes.

Salmon Sting Stew

Ingredients:

7 strips bacon
2 cups onion, chopped
7 potatoes, diced

2 stalks celery, roughly chopped
2 bay leaves
2 cups beefsteak tomatoes, peeled, chopped
2 cups morel mushrooms, chopped
2 cups fresh salmon, skinned, boned, cubed
½ teaspoon crushed red-pepper flakes
1 cup stinging nettles, steamed (Optional: See NOTE)
1½ cups white wine
Salt and pepper (to taste)

Directions:

Fry bacon.

Remove from pan and drain on paper towels; set aside.

Cook onion in bacon drippings until tender; set aside.

In a pot, cover potatoes and celery with water.

Add bay leaves.

Lid the pot.

Bring to boil.

Turn down heat to low.

Simmer covered until done.

Remove lid.

Crumble in bacon.

Add tomatoes, mushrooms, salmon, and red-pepper flakes.

Add nettles.

Add onions.

Add wine.

Stir.

Remove bay leaves before serving.

NOTE: In order to include nettles, you'll likely have to go out and collect them yourself. Be very careful when handling, because their small thorns can be extreme irritants. Rinse in strainer or colander, and then place in a steamer (DO NOT BOIL). Once steamed, they're easily handled and chopped.

Savory Lamb Stew

Ingredients:

1½ pounds lamb, cubed
2 Tablespoons olive oil
3 large onions, chopped
1 clove garlic, finely chopped
3 medium carrots, chopped
20 raisins
4 small potatoes, peeled, cubed
1½ cups beef broth
⅛ teaspoon NapaStyle® gray sea salt
¼ teaspoon pepper
2 Tablespoons butter
1 Tablespoon all-purpose flour
1½ teaspoons parsley, fresh, minced
½ teaspoon thyme, fresh, minced
¼ teaspoon ginger

¼ teaspoon red pepper
¼ teaspoon rosemary
¼ teaspoon clove, ground
½ teaspoon fennel, fresh, chopped
1 cup feta cheese, crumbled

Directions:

Brown lamb in 1 Tablespoon oil, over medium heat; set aside.

Sauté onions, garlic, carrots, and raisins in the remaining oil.

Cook for 5 minutes (or until onions are tender), stirring occasionally.

Add lamb, potatoes, broth, salt, and pepper.

Bring to a boil.

Remove from the heat.

Add butter, flour, parsley, thyme, ginger, red pepper, rosemary clove, and fennel.

Cook in preheated 350° oven 50-60 minutes (or until meat and vegetables are tender).

Remove from oven.

Sprinkle with feta cheese.

Venison Stew

Ingredients:

2 pounds venison, smoked, cubed
1 onion, chopped
3 cups Vegetable Stock (see Recipe for Vegetable Stock)
2 parsnips, chopped
3 potatoes, cubed
3 carrots, cubed
½ rutabaga, peeled, cubed
3 pears, firm, ripe, peeled, cored, cubed
3 Roma tomatoes, peeled, cubed
½ head cabbage, medium, coarsely chopped
1 bay leaf
½ teaspoon oregano, dried
⅛ teaspoon liquid smoke
1 teaspoon NapaStyle® gray sea salt
½ teaspoon white pepper
¼ cup Madeira wine

Directions:

Cook venison, onions, and Vegetable Stock in a large pot over medium heat for 30 minutes.

Add parsnip, potatoes, carrots, rutabaga, pears, tomatoes, cabbage, bay leaf, oregano, liquid smoke, salt, pepper, and Madeira wine, and mix.

Turn heat to high and bring to boil.

Reduce heat and simmer for 1½ hours (or until vegetables/fruits are soft); remove bay leaf before serving.

SOUPS

Avocado Soup

Ingredients:

2 large ripe avocados, pitted
1 cup apples, peeled, diced
1 cup plain yogurt
½ teaspoon hot sauce
¼ teaspoon NapaStyle® gray sea salt.
1 teaspoon lavender spice
½ cup celery, stringed, chopped
1 cup endive, chopped
1 cup zucchini, peeled, sliced
1 cup coconut meat, raw, chopped

Directions:

In blender, purée avocados, apples.

Add yogurt, hot sauce, salt, lavender spice, celery, endive, zucchini, coconut meat.

Purée.

Refrigerate.

Beef Cajun Soup

Ingredients:

1 pound red meat, cubed
3 cups water
1 large onion, chopped
6 Roma tomatoes, peeled, de-seeded, chopped
½ green pepper; chopped
2 garlic cloves, minced
2 cups beefsteak tomatoes, peeled, de-seeded, stewed, puréed
1 cup corn, cooked
1 cup okra, cooked
¼ cup black rice, cooked
¼ cup brown rice, cooked
2 Tablespoon Cajun Spice (see Recipe for Cajun Spice)
Salt & pepper

Directions:

In a large pan, put meat, water, onion, chopped Roma tomatoes, green pepper, garlic, and puréed beefcake tomatoes.

Simmer until meat has cooked through and through (about 60 minutes).

Add corn, okra, black rice, brown rice, Cajun Spice.

Cook 2½ hours on medium-to-low heat.

Salt and pepper to taste.

Bleuet Persil

Ingredients:

3 cups blueberries, fresh, rinsed (or flash frozen. defrosted)
3 cups parsley, raw, fresh, finely chopped
2 mint leaves, finely chopped
2¼ cups Vegetable Stock (See Recipe for Vegetable Stock)
½ cup sugar-free apple juice
¼ cup lemon juice, freshly squeezed
⅛ teaspoon nutmeg, ground
⅛ teaspoon salt
¼ teaspoon black pepper
1 cup pear pulp
1 Tablespoon lemon zest
2 teaspoons cardamom, ground
½ teaspoon garlic, ground
2 Tablespoons honey
3 Tablespoons white wine

Directions:

In a blender, put berries, parsley, and mint.

Purée.

While puréeing, slowly add 1⅛ cup Vegetable Stock, ¼ apple juice, and ⅛ cup lemon juice.

Add nutmeg, salt, pepper, pear pulp, lemon zest, cardamom, garlic.

Continue purée until ingredients finely mixed.

Pour into pan.

On medium-heat, bring to simmer (DO NOT BOIL).

Remove from heat.

Put in bowl.

Refrigerate for 24 hours.

Before serving, pour into pan.

Put on medium heat and bring to simmer (DO NOT BOIL).

Add honey and white wine.

NOTE: Done right, there will be a thin layer of vegetable matter floating the top.

Doux Orange-Potatoe-le Maïs et la Soupe

Ingredients:

7 cups water
2 cups sweet potatoes, cubed
2 cups sweet-corn kernels, cut from cob
4 cups orange juice, freshly squeezed
1 teaspoon ginger, fresh, minced
6 whole mint leaves, plus 4 mint leaves, finely chopped
½ cup cream
NapaStyle® gray sea salt and white pepper to taste

Directions:

In a pan on high heat, boil 5 cups of water, sweet potatoes, and corn until vegetables soft.

Drain, rinse vegetables.

Add juice, and 2 cups water.

Add ginger, and chopped mint (not whole leaves).

Bring to boil.

Turn down heat.

Simmer for 30 minutes.

Add cream, stirring slowly.

Salt and pepper to taste.

Garnish with whole mint leaves.

Fagus Nut Soup

Beech nuts are hard to find, need be roasted, and should NEVER be eaten raw.

Ingredients:

¾ cup sliced Fagus (beech) nuts, peeled, roasted, chopped
1 extra-virgin olive oil
3 cups water
1 large onion, sliced, sautéed
¾ teaspoon NapaStyle® gray sea salt
10 medium Roma tomatoes, peeled, diced
1 teaspoon oregano

Directions:

In sauté pan, on medium heat, sauté nuts in olive oil until brown and tender; set aside.

In saucepan, combine water, onion, and salt.

Bring to boil.

Reduce heat.

Add nuts, tomatoes, and oregano.

Cook for 5-10 minutes (until tomato is desired consistency).

Hot...Red...Neck...Soup

Ingredients:

3 turkey necks
½ pound stew meat, cubed, chopped
2 persimmons, peeled, chopped
2 quince, peeled, chopped
2 cups collard greens, cleaned, de-stemmed
3 whole okra, chopped into little roundettes
1½ cup black-eyed peas, soaked 24 hours
1 hot red pepper, de-seeded, chopped
1 cup corn
1 white onion, cubed
1 cup white hominy
2 pimientos, chopped
1 cup beer
2 cups water
½ teaspoon NapaStyle® gray sea salt
½ teaspoon oregano

½ teaspoon basil
½ teaspoon chives

Directions:

Boil turkey necks until meat comes off bone.

Discard chicken necks; save water.

In a sauce pan, brown stew meat; set aside.

Bring turkey water to soft boil.

Add remaining ingredients (but not stew meat).

Cook down to soft consistency.

Add the stew meat.

Simmer for 10 minutes.

Mushroom Apple Soup

Ingredients:

1½ cups water
8 small red apples, peeled, cored, cubed
1 pound shitake mushrooms, chopped
½ cup raisins, chopped
½ teaspoon oregano
½ teaspoon walnut extract
3 drops hot sauce
½ teaspoon Cajun Spice (see Recipe for Cajun Spice)
⅛ teaspoon NapaStyle® gray sea salt
½ teaspoon white pepper

⅛ teaspoon chili pepper
½ cup apple juice

Directions:

In pot, on high heat, bring water to roiling boil.

Turn down heat to low.

Add cubed apples, mushrooms, raisins, oregano, walnut extract, hot sauce, Cajun Spice, sea salt, white pepper, chili pepper, apple juice.

Simmer 30 minutes.

Serve cold or hot.

Pineapple Pumpkin Soup

Ingredients:

½ cup white onion, diced
½ cup water
2 teaspoons chicken bouillon
16 ounces pumpkin, fresh
2½ cups half-and-half
1 cup pineapple juice
¾ cup crushed pineapple
¼ teaspoon ginger, ground
¼ teaspoon nutmeg, ground
¼ teaspoon white pepper

Directions:

In large saucepan, on high heat, combine onion, water, and

bouillon.

Bring to a boil.

Turn to low heat, and simmer, covered, for 10 minutes (or until onion is tender).

Cool slightly.

Transfer mixture to blender.

Add pumpkin.

Cover blender top with cloth and blend.

Pour blend into saucepan on medium heat.

Stir in half-and-half, pineapple juice, crushed pineapple, ginger, nutmeg, and pepper.

Heat through.

Sour White Grape Soup

Ingredients:

1 pound white (green) grapes, de-seeded, stemmed.
2-3 cucumbers, peeled, de-seeded
2 cups plain sugar-free yogurt
1 cup sour cream
⅛ teaspoon almond extract
1 mild chili pepper, stemmed, de-seeded.
2 shallots, finely chopped
1 clove garlic, minced
1 teaspoon lime

1 clove, ground
NapaStyle® gray sea salt and pepper to taste

Directions:

With a sharp knife, engrave a cross in each grape.

Put grapes in boiling water for 20 seconds.

Drain.

Blanch in cold water.

Peel grapes.

Put in blender.

Add all other ingredients.

Purée.

Chill for half an hour.

Squash Berry Soup

Ingredients:

2 cups white or yellow hominy, drained
2 cups green beans, fresh, finely chopped
2 cups butternut squash, peeled, cubed
1½ cup red potatoes, diced, peeled
5 cups water
1½ Tablespoons Vegetable Stock (see Recipe for Vegetable Stock)
1 cup raspberries

1 cup blackberries
½ Basic Roux (see Recipe for Basic Roux)
¼ teaspoon pepper (or to taste)

Directions:

In a pot, put hominy, green beans, squash, and potatoes.

Add water and Vegetable Stock.

On high heat, bring to a boil.

Turn down heat to low.

Simmer until vegetables are soft (about 10 minutes).

Add raspberries and blackberries, squishing them as you do.

Simmer.

Add Basic Roux.

Increase heat to medium.

Cook 5 minutes (or until soup sufficiently thickens).

Pepper to taste.

Sunshine Soup

Ingredients:

1 cup walnuts (puréed to fine powder)
2 Tablespoons butter
4 chicken breasts, boneless

¼ teaspoon garlic, diced
1 big squeeze of lemon
10 mushrooms, chopped
2 leeks, chopped
2 Tablespoons pineapple, diced
2 Tablespoons cherries, peeled, de-seeded, diced
2 cups cream (NOT MILK)
1 cup water
⅛ teaspoon walnut butter
⅛ teaspoon ginger
⅛ teaspoon cardamom

Directions:

Mix walnut powder and 1 Tablespoon butter to make paste; set aside.

Boil chicken until oil sits water.

Skim off oil and discard.

Discard water.

Cut chicken into bite-size pieces.

Braise in sauté pan until crusty; transfer to plate.

In sauté pan, put garlic, 1 Tablespoon butter, and lemon juice.

Add mushrooms, leeks, pineapple, and cherries.

Toss.

Sauté (add drops of water to keep from going jelly).

As soon as mushrooms are soft, pour into blender.

Add chicken.

Purée (See NOTE).

Pour purée into sauce pan on medium-high heat.

Add cream, water, walnut butter, ginger, cardamom.

Stir while brining mixture to GENTLE boil.

NOTE: Blenders can cause a vacuum with hot foods to cause splatter and burns; so don't put the top on completely, and/or put a towel over the top.

Tropical Creamed Asparagus Soup

Ingredients:

1 cups white grapes, de-seeded, stemmed
1 Tablespoon butter
3 medium spring onions (DO NOT USE GREEN), cleaned, diced
2 cups ounces asparagus, remove hard ends
1 Tablespoon Italian parsley, fresh, chopped
1 Tablespoon zest from one lemon
5 cups Vegetable Stock (see Recipe for Vegetable Stock)
2 cups starchy rice
1 cup Parmesan cheese, fresh, grated
1 cup dry white wine
1 cup heavy cream
1 Tablespoon lemon juice, fresh, squeezed
⅛ teaspoon NapaStyle® gray sea salt
⅛ teaspoon black pepper

Directions

With a sharp knife, engrave a cross in each grape.

Put grapes in boiling water for 20 seconds.

Drain.

Blanch in cold water.

Peel grapes; set aside.

In sauté pan, put butter, and sauté the onions, asparagus, parsley, and zest.

Stir to keep from burning.

Let cool.

Put in blender and purée.

Add grapes.

Purée; set aside.

Boil Vegetable Stock.

Add rice.

Once rice is soft (DON'T OVER-BOIL), strain off stock into separate bowl; set aside.

Put rice in blender and purée.

Return rice to Vegetable Stock.

In a saucepan, on medium-heat, bring to near boiling.

Stir in Parmesan cheese.

Stir in wine.

Turn down heat to low.

Stir in cream.

Stir in lemon juice.

Add salt and pepper to taste.

Vegetable Stock

Ingredients:

1 gallon of water
1 teaspoon of NapaStyle® gray sea salt
1 teaspoon of white pepper
2-3 garlic cloves, cleaned, not peeled, chopped
2 onions, not peeled, cleaned, chopped
1 celery stalk, not peeled, cleaned, chopped
1 carrot, not peeled, cleaned, chopped
1 mushroom, not peeled, cleaned, chopped
1 bell pepper, not peeled, cleaned, chopped
1 parsnip, not peeled, cleaned, chopped
1 spinach leaf, cleaned, chopped
1 leek, not peeled, cleaned, chopped
1 turnip, not peeled, cleaned, chopped
1 zucchini, not peeled, cleaned, chopped
1 tomato (see NOTE)
Vegetable leftovers, cleaned, chopped—potato peel, broccoli and cauliflower stems, green bean ends...

Directions:

Put all vegetables into large pot.

On high heat, bring to a boil.

Turn down heat and simmer until all vegetables are completely broken down.

Strain.

NOTE: Add tomato for a minestrone-base broth.

NOTE: Strained and puréed vegetables can be warmed up to be used for dog or cat food; lasts 4 days when chilled.

SALADS

Bacon & Broccoli Salad

Ingredients:

2 Tablespoons lemon juice
2 Tablespoon olive oil
2 Tablespoons balsamic vinegar
4 cloves of garlic, minced
1 teaspoon mustard
½ teaspoon NapaStyle® gray sea salt
½ teaspoon white pepper
1 teaspoon chili flakes
1 head of broccoli
1 cup walnuts, chopped
1 cup huckleberries
4 strips of bacon, cooked, crumbled

Directions:

In a small bowl, whisk lemon juice, olive oil, vinegar, garlic, mustard, salt, pepper, and chili flakes.

Refrigerate.

Chop broccoli.

Boil broccoli 10-15 minutes (NOT UNTIL BROWN).

Douse in cold water.

Drain and dry.

Put in large bowl.

Toss with walnuts and huckleberries.

Chill.

Cook bacon until brown.

Drain.

Crumble; put aside.

Toss chilled salad with chilled dressing.

Sprinkle on crumbled bacon.

Bearlee Salad

Ingredients

8 Roma tomatoes, chopped
4 Tablespoons non-alcoholic red wine
3 pints (6 cups) raspberries
½ teaspoon rubbed lemon grass
⅛ teaspoon horseradish
4 white radishes, finely chopped
½ teaspoon poppy seeds
2 teaspoons honey, warm
2 small wild onions (or shallots) finely chopped

Directions:

Gently mix all ingredients in a large serving bowl.

Refrigerate.

(Black) Red Radish Roast Chunky Vegetable Aperitif

Ingredients:

10 raspberries
½ teaspoon sugar
3 sprigs of parsley, finely
¼ teaspoon white pepper
⅛ teaspoon NapaStyle® gray sea salt
10 radishes, chopped
1 teaspoon olive oil
1 teaspoon white wine

Directions:

In a medium bowl, crush raspberries.

Add sugar, parsley, pepper, and salt.

Stir and set aside.

Blanch radishes for 3 minutes.

Grate.

Add crushed raspberries to grated radishes.

Add olive oil and mix.

Stir in wine.

Serve cold.

Chocolate Hot Pepper Salad

Ingredients:

2 teaspoons extra-light olive oil
2 Tablespoons raspberry vinegar
3 Tablespoons orange juice, fresh, squeezed
4 Tablespoons Sangiovese wine
1 cup cherry-bomb hybrid peppers, rinsed, de-seeded, chopped
¼ cup cherries, dried, finely chopped
½ cup raspberries
1 cup pistachio nuts, chopped
¼ cup pine nuts
1 cup feta cheese, thinly crumbled
1 cup semi-sweet chocolate, grated

Directions:

In a blender, blend olive oil, vinegar, orange juice, wine.

Refrigerate.

In a small bowl, toss peppers, cherries, raspberries, and nuts (pistachio and pine).

Add chilled dressing.

Toss.

Sprinkle feta cheese, and sprinkle chocolate.

Flavor of Africa Salad

Ingredients:

1 avocado, peeled, de-seeded
1 banana
1 grapefruit, peeled, de-seeded, cubed
1 guava, peeled, de-seeded, cubed
1 mango, peeled, de-seeded, cubed
1 melon, peeled, de-seeded, cubed
1 orange, peeled, de-seeded, cubed
1 papaya, peeled, de-seeded, cubed
1 peach, peeled, de-seeded, cubed
1 pear, peeled, de-seeded, cubed
1 tangerine, peeled, de-seeded, cubed
1 pineapple, peeled, de-seeded, cubed
Juice of 1 lemon
3 mint leaves, chopped, crushed
1 teaspoon African Spice (see Recipe for African Spice)
3 Tablespoons honey
Coconut, grated
1 cup peanuts, roasted, chopped

Directions:

In a large glass bowl, combine all cubed fruit.

Add the lemon juice, mint, African Spice, and honey.

Mix.

Cover.

Let stand at room temperature for 1 hr.

Serve (or refrigerate)

Sprinkle with grated coconut.

Sprinkle with nuts.

Garden Tuna Salad

Ingredients:

2 cups tuna, fresh, cubed
2 Tablespoons olive oil
Salt to taste
Pepper to taste
2 cups alfalfa sprouts, finely diced
3 red apples, diced
2 hard-boiled, eggs, finely diced
1 cup walnuts, finely chopped
½ cup raisins
½ cup cranberries, dried
½ cup celery, finely diced
½ carrots, finely diced
½ cup capers
½ cup red cabbage, finely chopped
1 tomato, finely diced
8 black olives, finely diced
¼ cucumber, finely diced
¼ cup lemon juice, fresh
1 teaspoon curry
½ teaspoon ginger
3 Tablespoons Parmesan cheese
½ teaspoon poppy seeds
½ teaspoon sesame seeds
⅓ cup Oro Marsala

Directions:

In a pan, cook tuna in olive oil, salt, and pepper.

Drain.

Refrigerate.

In a large bowl, gently combine sprouts, apples, eggs, walnuts, raisins, cranberries, celery, carrots, capers, cabbage, tomato, olives, cucumber, lemon juice, curry, ginger, cheese, poppy seeds, sesame seeds, and Oro Marsala.

Refrigerate.

2 hours before serving, gently add and fold in tuna.

Serve chilled.

Mediterranean Snapper Salad

Ingredients:

1 teaspoon butter
¼ teaspoon tarragon, ground
2 red snapper fillets, scaled, boned
2 guavas, peeled, de-seeded, diced
2 tangerines, peeled, de-seeded, chopped
3 green apples, chopped
2 avocados, peeled, de-seeded, diced
3 cups red grapes, halved
¼ red onion, chopped
1 Tablespoon Mediterranean Spice (see Recipe for Mediterranean Spice)
1 teaspoon cardamom

1 cup Pear Crème (see Recipe for Pear Crème)
⅛ teaspoon NapaStyle® gray sea salt
⅛ teaspoon white pepper
Zest from 1 lemon
Juice from 1 lemon

Directions:

In small bowl, mix butter and tarragon.

Smear butter/tarragon mixture on fish fillet, skin-side.

Broil fillets in oven, skin-side up, until done.

Cut fillets into pieces; set aside.

In medium bowl, toss guavas, tangerines, apples, avocados, grapes, onion, Mediterranean Spice, cardamom, Pear Crème, salt, pepper, zest, juice.

Add fish.

Refrigerate.

Serve chilled.

Strawberry Minced Meat Salad

Ingredients:

1 Tablespoon flax seeds
2 Tablespoons sesame seeds
1 Tablespoon poppy seeds
2 Tablespoons sunflower seeds
¼ cup white sugar

¼ cup olive oil
¼ cup balsamic vinegar
¼ teaspoon saffron
10 ounces spinach, fresh, rinsed, dried de-stemmed, torn in small pieces
1 quart strawberries, cleaned, hulled, quartered
4 dates, chopped
¼ cup almonds, blanched, slivered
½ cup Black Forest ham, cooked, finely chopped
½ cup venison, cooked, finely chopped
½ cup roast beef, cooked, finely chopped
½ cup turkey, cooked, finely chopped

Directions:

In a medium bowl, whisk flax, sesame, poppy, and sunflower seeds, with sugar, olive oil, vinegar, and saffron.

Cover.

Refrigerate for 1 hr.

In a large bowl, combine spinach, strawberries, dates, almonds, ham, venison, roast, and turkey.

Add chilled dressing.

Toss.

Refrigerate 10 to 15 minutes.

Serve.

Tomato & Shrimp Aspic

Ingredients:

5 cups tomato juice
3 small packages lemon gelatin
1 cup shrimp, finely chopped
½ teaspoon garlic clove, minced
3 teaspoons horseradish
2 Tablespoons lemon juice
Celery, finely chopped
Mint, finely chopped
⅛ teaspoon sage, ground
⅛ teaspoon ginger fresh, ground
2 Tablespoons whiskey
⅛ teaspoon clove, ground

Directions:

In a pot, heat tomato juice to boil.

Pour into heat resistant bowl.

Stir in gelatin.

Add shrimp, garlic, horseradish, lemon juice, celery, mint, sage, ginger, whiskey, clove.

Stir.

Refrigerate; when jelled, cut into uniform pieces.

Serve by turning pieces so the heavier sunken ingredients are on top.

"Weeds" Salad

In case you're wondering, the "weeds" in "Weeds" Salad doesn't really mean "weeds".

Ingredients:
¼ cup sherry
¼ cup olive oil
⅛ teaspoon NapaStyle® gray sea salt
¼ teaspoon white pepper
¼ cup balsamic Vinegar
½ cup arugula
½ cup beet greens
½ cup bok choy
½ cup butter lettuce
½ cup spinach
½ cup red leaf-lettuce
½ cup green-leaf lettuce
½ cup Mesclun
½ cup mache
½ cup mizuna
½ cup Romaine hearts
½ cup watercress leaves
½ cup asparagus leaves
½ cup fennel
¼ cup sunflower seeds, roasted
¼ cup almonds, roasted
¼ cup raisins
¼ cup cranberries, dried

Directions:

In a blender, blend sherry, olive oil, salt, white pepper, and balsamic vinegar.

Put in spritzer.

Refrigerate.

Wash all of the mentioned greens well.

Pull all leaves from all heads, but don't cut.

Remove all of the stems from the leaves.

Place greens in large bowl.

Add sunflower seeds, almonds, raisins, and cranberries.

Spritz lightly with chilled dressing.

Wild Violets and Riesling Salad

Ingredients:

4 teaspoons maple syrup
1 teaspoon lemon juice, fresh
½ cup Riesling
1 cup red leaf lettuce, chopped
1 cup curly radicchio lettuce, chopped
2 cups watercress, chopped
1 cup spinach, leaves pulled, stalks removed, chopped
2 cups violets, picked, rinsed
1 cup Asiago cheese, grated
1 cup almonds, sliced

Directions

In small bowl, whisk syrup, juice, and wine.

Refrigerate.

In large bowl, toss both lettuces, watercress, and spinach.

Add violets, cheese, and almonds.

Toss.

Add a chilled dressing.

Toss.

Yellow Beets Red Salad

Ingredients:

½ pound yellow beets
1 large shallot, thinly sliced
2 Tablespoons lemon juice, fresh
1 teaspoon Oriental Spice (see Recipe for Oriental Spice)
½ cup extra-virgin olive oil
3 Tablespoons white wine
½ teaspoon NapaStyle® gray sea salt
½ teaspoon black pepper, freshly ground
4 cups arugula, washed, dried
½ cup feta cheese, crumbled
¼ cup mint leaves, fresh
½ cup pistachios

Directions:

Wrap beets and shallots in foil.

Roast in preheated 400° oven 1 hour (or until tender).

Remove and cool.

In small measuring cup, whisk lemon juice, Oriental Spice, oil, wine, salt, and pepper.

Unwrap cooked shallots and beets.

Peel cooked beets and discard skins.

In a bowl, toss cooked shallots and cooked beets with ½ of the measuring-cup contents.

Set aside.

In a bowl, toss arugula with remaining measuring-cup contents.

Plate beets and shallots in the center of arugula.

Scatter on cheese, mint, and pistachios.

Serve.

SIDE DISHES

Gardenia Zucchini

Ingredients:

2 Tablespoons butter
2 zucchini, thinly sliced
1 tomato chopped fine
1 garlic clove minced
2 gardenia leaves, chopped fine
1 wiggle (1/16 teaspoon) NapaStyle® gray sea salt
1 pinch white pepper

Directions:

In a pan with butter, lightly brown zucchini, first one side, then the other side.

Add chopped tomatoes, minced garlic, and gardenia leaves.

Cook until vegetables are soft, stirring frequently.

Add salt and pepper serve hot.

Serves 4.

Mexican Rice

Ingredients:

2 Tablespoons oil
¼ of a medium onion
1½ cups rice
3 cloves finely chopped garlic
2½ cups vegetable broth
1 cup puréed tomatoes, but skin them first and get rid of the seeds
1 Tablespoon Mexican Spice
4 heaping Tablespoons of finely chopped parsley

Directions:

In a medium sauce pan, heat oil over medium heat.

Add in the fresh onion, and sauté for 2 minutes or until softened.

Add dry rice and cook with the onions for about 5 minutes, or until rice becomes a golden brown color.

Add garlic to the rice and sauté for one more minute.

Add broth and tomato purée and spice.

Add parsley.

Stir and bring to a boil.

Once it starts boiling, turn the heat to low and cover.

Let it simmer for 20 minutes, and fluff with a fork.

Minced Vegetarian Menagerie

Ingredients:

½ cup raisins, minced
½ cup cucumber, minced
½ cup strawberries, minced
½ cup celery, minced
½ cup mushrooms, minced
½ cup radishes, minced
½ cup cress, minced
½ cup beet greens, minced
½ cup kale, minced
½ cup turnip, minced
½ cup avocado, minced
½ cup tomato, minced
½ cup garbanzo beans, minced
½ cup cooked peas, minced
1 cup water
1 Tablespoon butter
1 teaspoon rice flour
1 wiggle (1/16 teaspoon) NapaStyle® gray sea salt

Directions:

In a sauté pan mix everything together and brown quickly on high heat.

Stir constantly.

Lower the heat to simmer for 5 minutes, then let stand on the burner after you turn off the heat.

Serve while hot; serves 6.

Roasted Asparagus

Spicy dishes go well with mild-flavored meats or salads.

Ingredients:

2 bundles fresh asparagus
1 Tablespoon butter
1 wiggle (1/16 teaspoon) NapaStyle® gray sea salt
¼ teaspoon The Heart of Spokane William Maltese Hottie Spice Mix (can be purchased at www.theheartofspokane.com)
⅓ cup pine nuts, puréed
⅓ cup chopped parsley
Zest from one lemon

Directions:

Toss trimmed and chopped asparagus with butter, salt, and The Heart of Spokane William Maltese Hottie Spice Mix, and spread on a baking sheet.

Roast at 450° F. until browned (about 15 minutes). Remove from oven.

Mix puréed pine nuts; parsley, and lemon zest together and sprinkle over asparagus, then serve.

Serves 4.

Tomato Pecan Green Beans

Ingredients:

3 cups fresh green beans
1 cup water
1 cup chicken broth
1 Tablespoon butter
½ teaspoon natural sugar
¼ teaspoon clove, ground
¼ teaspoon ginger, ground
1 Roma tomato, peeled, seeded, and chopped
½ cup pecans, finely chopped

Directions:

Snap the ends off the green beans, pull the strings out of the green bean seams, and cut into uniform pieces.

Place green beans in simmering water and chicken broth.

Once soft (about 12 minutes), drain and add butter and sugar and seasonings.

Sauté green beans with the tomato and pecans until coated and turning brown.

Serves 4.

Vanilla Pansy Butternut Squash

Ingredients:

1 butternut squash, about 2 pounds, peeled, seeds removed, and cut into 1-inch cubes.
3 Tablespoons butter
1 wiggle (1/16 teaspoon) NapaStyle® gray Sea Salt
1 heaping cup of walnuts
2 teaspoons grated ginger
2 teaspoons vanilla extract
Black pepper to taste
1 wiggle (1/16 teaspoon) of NapaStyle® gray sea salt
½ teaspoon dried thyme
1 cup pansies chopped
1 whole lemon squeezed into lemon juice

Directions:

Preheat oven to 400°F.

Coat the cubed squash with a little butter and spread out onto a baking tray. Sprinkle with salt and roast until the cubes begin to brown (about 20 minutes). Remove from oven and set aside.

Heat a large sauté pan over medium-high heat and toast the walnuts. Stir frequently or they will burn. Once they start to brown, and the aroma is heavy, remove from heat.

Melt the butter in the pan with the walnuts over medium-high heat. Toss walnuts to coat with butter.

Add squash. Toss both to coat with butter.

Add the grated ginger, vanilla extract, black pepper, salt, dried thyme, and pansies. Toss.

Turn off the heat and pour the fresh squeezed lemon juice over everything.

Taste for salt and lemon, and add more to taste.

Serves 4.

Vegetarian Gratinée

Ingredients:

1 Tablespoon butter
3 new (red) potatoes, peeled and cubed
1 cup broccoli, cubed
1 cup carrots, cubed
1 cup heavy cream
½ cup water
4 cloves garlic, minced
2 Tablespoons millet flour
1 wiggle (1/16 teaspoon) NapaStyle® gray sea salt
1 dash (1/16 teaspoon) pepper
1 cup grated Havarti cheese
3 cups finely chopped almonds

Directions:

Preheat an oven to 350° F.

Grease one 9" x 13" baking pan with butter. Spread potatoes, broccoli, and carrots evenly in the pan. Set aside.

In a large bowl, whisk together heavy cream, water, garlic, flour, salt, and pepper.

Pour cream mixture over the vegetables. Cover with foil.

Bake for 20 minutes, and then remove the foil.

Continue baking until the potatoes are easily pierced with a fork (about 40 minutes).

Remove from the oven and sprinkle Havarti cheese.

Return to oven and bake until the cheese is melted; then top tightly with finely chopped almonds, and cook an additional 5-10 minutes (until brown).

Remove from oven and allow cooling for 5 minutes.

Serves 4.

NOTE: This can be a gluten-free recipe, if you decide to use Crystal Farms gluten-free Havarti cheese, as well as the non-gluten millet flour.

Wild Rice e Trito di Verdure

Ingredients:

1 cup wild rice
3 cups water
2 wiggles (⅛ teaspoon) NapaStyle® gray sea salt
1 Tablespoon butter
¼ cup tomatoes, sun-dried and finely chopped
¼ cup Italian parsley (do not substitute), finely chopped
¼ cup shallots, finely chopped
¼ cup mushrooms, finely chopped
¼ cup green onions, finely chopped
1 teaspoon Italian seasoning (see Italian seasoning)

1 teaspoon virgin olive oil

Directions:

In a medium saucepan, bring wild rice, 3 cups water, and 1 wiggle (1/16 teaspoon) of salt to a boil. Cover and reduce heat to maintain a steady simmer.

Cook rice until tender and kernels pop (45-60 minutes).

Uncover rice and fluff with a fork.

Simmer rice 5 additional minutes, stirring occasionally. Set aside.

Add butter to a sauté pan with all the chopped vegetables, the second 1 wiggle (1/16 teaspoon) of salt, and the Italian seasoning. Sauté.

Pat sautéed vegetables dry with a paper towel.

In a large bowl, toss rice, sautéed vegetables, and virgin olive oil.

Serve immediately.

Serves 2.

Wilted Spinach and Broccoli

Ingredients:

8 cups spinach
1 head broccoli florets, rinsed and cut into ½-inch pieces
1 Tablespoon fresh lime juice

1 Tablespoon butter
1 Tablespoon honey
Zest of 1 whole lime
1 Tablespoon black pepper, ground
1 wiggle (1/16 teaspoon) NapaStyle® gray sea salt
½ cup water

Directions:

Wash and paper-towel pat dry the spinach, then pull all the stems out of the middle of each leaf. Place spinach to one side.

Simmer broccoli in a pan of water for 6 minutes (or until softened); do not let their color turn brown. Strain off water, toss with lemon juice (to keep green color), and then set broccoli aside.

In a medium sauté pan, brown the butter, and then add honey, zest of lime, pepper, and salt.

Add the spinach and broccoli florets into the sauté pan. and sauté until spinach is coated.

Add ½ cup of water and cover with lid until the spinach droops.

Serve hot.

Serves 4.

DESSERTS

Apricot Nectar Cake

Ingredients:

24 apricots, diced
Angel Food Cake (see Recipe for Angel Food Cake), torn into bite-sized bits
1 cup coconut, finely grated
1 Tablespoon cornstarch
1½ cup sugar

Directions:

In a pot, reduce 24 apricots to slush.

Run through sieve for approximately 46 ounces of nectar; separate nectar from pulp; set aside.

In a mixing bowl, combine Angel Food Cake bits and coconut.

Spoon into 9" x 13" greased glass baking dish.

Spoon on layer of apricot pulp.

In a sauce pan, over medium heat, combine nectar, cornstarch, and sugar.

Cook until clear and bubbly, watching closely,

Remove from heat.

Pour over layered fruit pulp and cake bits in baking dish.

Cover.

Refrigerate for 24 hours.

Basic White Cake

Ingredients:

2 eggs
1 cup white sugar
½ cup butter
2 teaspoons vanilla extract
1½ cups all-purpose flour
1¾ teaspoons baking powder
½ cup milk

Directions:

Preheat oven 350°.

Butter and flour 9" x 9" cake pan

In a large bowl, beat eggs, sugar, and butter.

Add vanilla extract; set aside.

In a medium bowl, combine flour and baking powder.

Add flour/baking powder mixture to egg/sugar/butter mixture.

Mix well.

Stir in milk until batter is smooth.

Pour into cake pan.

Bake for 30-40 minutes (or until done).

Loosen cake by running sharp knife along pan's edges.

Turn cake carefully onto serving plate.

Ciliegie Fritte

Ingredients:

Almond Crème (see Recipe for Almond Crème)
Dusting + ½ teaspoon nutmeg, ground
Mint leaves, washed, dried
2 cups all-purpose flour
¼ cup white sugar
1 Tablespoon baking powder
1 teaspoon salt
2 eggs
¾ cup heavy cream
¼ cup Amaretto
Butter and oil
4 cups fresh cherries, with strong stems, washed, dried, pitted

Directions:

Smear each serving plate with Almond Crème.

Dust with nutmeg.

Position mint leaves.

In a medium bowl, mix flour, sugar, baking powder, ½ teaspoon nutmeg, and salt; set aside.

In a medium bowl, mix eggs, cream, and Amaretto.

Add cream mixture to flour mixture.

Stir until smooth; set aside.

In a heavy-bottomed skillet, heat enough butter and oil to fry batter-dipped cherries.

Dip each cherry in batter, almost to the stem.

Place cherries, one at a time in butter and oil.

Fry, trying to keep stems in air, until cherries are golden brown.

Place on serving plates.

Coconut Rum Cheese Pie

Ingredients:

Pie Crust (see Recipe for Pie Crust)
2 cups coconut, grated, fresh, roasted, crumbled
⅓ cup butter, soft
½ cup sugar
⅓ cup sour cream
⅓ cup cream cheese
2 eggs, beaten
⅔ cup heavy cream
⅓ cup Golden Rum

½ cup farmer cheese
1 teaspoon vanilla, real
⅛ teaspoon baking soda
½ teaspoon nutmeg, grated (optional)

Directions:

Make Pie Crust.

Roll out into two circles; set one to the side.

Line bottom of pie plate with one dough circle.

Punch fork holes in plated dough; set aside.

On a large flat cookie pan, broil coconut until brown; set aside.

In a large kitchen bowl, blend butter and sugar.

Slowly mix in sour cream, cream cheese, eggs, heavy cream, Golden Rum, farmer cheese, vanilla, baking soda, and (if desired) nutmeg.

Pour ingredients into pie pan.

Cover with second circle of pie dough.

Tamp down dough edges to seal.

Punch fork holes into top crust to provide steam venting.

Bake in preheated 350° oven 30-40 minutes (or until filling is done, crust golden.

Serve warm, or room temperature.

Golden Rhum Vanille Pudding

Ingredients:

½ cup sugar
2 Tablespoons cornstarch
⅛ teaspoon salt
1 cup whole milk
1 cup heavy cream
½ teaspoon lemon zest, grated
¼ cup fresh lemon juice (or to taste)
2 Tablespoons butter, unsalted, bits
1 egg yolk, large
⅛ teaspoon nutmeg
2 Tablespoons almonds, slivers
4 teaspoons rum

Directions:

In 1½ quart saucepan, combine sugar, cornstarch, and salt.

Slowly pour in milk, cream, and zest, until smooth.

Bring to a boil on medium heat, stirring constantly.

Continue stirring constantly for 2 minutes.

Remove from heat.

Add lemon juice, butter, nutmeg, and egg yolk.

Transfer pudding to bowl.

Add more lemon juice (if desired) to taste.

Cover visible surface with parchment paper.

Cool until thickened (about 120 minutes).

Spoon into individual serving plates.

Refrigerate 1 hour.

Top with rum.

Sprinkle with almonds.

Green Tomato Coffee Cake

Ingredients:

2¼ cups sugar
1 cup butter
3 eggs
2 teaspoons vanilla
3 cups flour
1 teaspoon salt
1 teaspoon baking powder
1 teaspoon cinnamon
½ teaspoon nutmeg
4 fresh coffee beans, finely ground
1 cup pecans, chopped
1 cup raisins, halved
2½ cups + 2 green tomatoes, diced
2 Tablespoons of brown sugar
2 Tablespoons Clarified Butter (see Recipe for Clarified Butter)
½ cup shredded coconut
½ teaspoon turmeric, ground

Directions:

Preheat oven to 350°.

Lightly butter and flour 9" x 13" glass baking dish.

In a bowl, beat sugar, butter, eggs, and vanilla, until smooth and creamy; set aside.

In a bowl sift flour, salt, baking powder, cinnamon, nutmeg, and coffee beans.

Slowly add egg mixture to flour mixture.

Mix well.

Add pecans, raisins, and 2½ cups diced tomatoes, and mix.

Pour batter into baking dish.

Bake in preheated 350° oven for 1 hour (or until done).

Let cool.

Slide sharp knife around circumference of cake.

Cover cake pan with serving dish.

Tip and tap lightly to transfer cake to plate; set aside.

In a sauce pan, over medium-low heat, combine 2 green diced tomatoes, brown sugar, Clarified Butter, coconut, and turmeric.

Stir constantly until jellied.

Spread atop cake.

Island Rum Cake

Ingredients:

1 cup almonds, slivers
1 cup mango, peeled, cubed
1 cup white sugar
2 eggs
2 teaspoons vanilla extract
1½ cups all-purpose flour
1¾ teaspoons baking powder
½ cup heavy cream
⅓ cup water
½ cup rum + extra for basting
½ cup ripe mango, puréed

Directions:

Preheat oven to 350°.

Butter and flour tube pan.

Put a single layer of almonds on bottom of pan.

Arrange mango cubes on almonds.

In a mixer, low speed, slowly combine, sugar, eggs, vanilla extract, flour, baking powder, heavy cream, water, rum, and puréed mango.

Increase speed to medium.

Mix 4 minutes.

Pour batter into pan.

Bake 40-45 minutes (or until done).

Cool 20 minutes in pan.

Loosen cake by running sharp knife along pan's edges.

Turn cake carefully onto serving plate.

Brush with extra rum.

Layered Blueberry Tort

Ingredients:

Pâté à Choux (see Recipe for Pâté à Choux—Puff Pastry)
4 Tablespoons flour
1 teaspoon vanilla extract
½ cup almonds + handful almonds, chopped
½ teaspoon nutmeg
½ teaspoon cinnamon
2 Tablespoons + ½ cup granular sugar
3 cups cream cheese
1 cup heavy cream
¼ Tablespoons powdered sugar
4 cups fresh blueberries, washed and dried

Directions

Preheated oven to 400°.

To Pâté à Choux, add 4 Tablespoons flour.

Mix well.

Add ¼ cup almonds, ½ teaspoon vanilla extract, nutmeg,

cinnamon, and 2 Tablespoons of sugar.

Mix well.

Divide into three.

Roll out three pie crusts to diameter of pie pan.

Cover large sheet pan with parchment paper.

Place rolled puff pastry on parchment.

Cook dough until golden brown (DO NOT BURN); set aside.

Cool.

In a bowl, combine softened cream cheese with ½ cup sugar.

Mix well.

Add ½ teaspoon vanilla.

Blend thoroughly; set aside.

In a bowl, beat heavy cream and powdered sugar until stiff.

Refrigerate.

Toast ¼ cup almonds; set aside.

In pie pan, form alternating layers of puff pastry, cream cheese mixture, blueberries, whipped cream, and toasted almonds, ending with a sprinkle of toasted almonds.

Freeze for 1 hour, and refrigerate until use.

Layered Floating Chocolate Hazelnut Brandy

Ingredients:

Meringue, eight servings, refrigerated (see Recipe for Meringue)
1 quart water
¼ baking soda
2 cups hazelnuts, shelled
½ cup cocoa powder, dark, unsweetened
1¼ cups powdered sugar
¼ teaspoon salt + to taste
3 Tablespoons Clarified Butter + possible extra (see Recipe for Clarified Butter)
8 teaspoons brandy
⅛ teaspoon nutmeg

Directions

Preheat oven to 350°.

In a pot, bring water and baking soda to boil.

Add hazelnuts.

Let boil 3-4 minutes.

Drain nuts into colander.

Run with cold water.

Remove skin from the nuts.

Arrange nuts on jellyroll pan in a single layer.

Push all nuts toward the center—stray nuts tend to burn.

Toast for 10-12 minutes.

Turn nuts.

Repeat toasting until nuts are evenly brown.

Put the toasted hazelnuts in food processor.

Grind to paste, then liquid.

Add cocoa, sugar, salt, and Clarified Butter.

Blend until smooth.

If too thick, add more butter.

If not salty enough, salt to taste.

Refrigerate.

To serve, hollow middles of Meringue.

Spoon chocolate/hazelnut mix into hollows.

Drizzle brandy.

Sprinkle nutmeg.

No-Cook Cheese Cake

Ingredients:

1½ cup graham crackers, crushed
⅓ cup butter
1 pint heavy whipping cream

1 package Knox gelatin
⅓ cup sugar
1 eight-ounce package cream cheese, soft
1 eight-ounce can sweetened condensed milk
Juice of 6 lemons, de-seeded, strained
zest of 1 lemon
¼ teaspoon almond extract

Directions:

Mix graham crackers, flour, and butter.

Press to line 9" pie pan.

Refrigerate.

In a mixing bowl, sprinkle gelatin over whipping cream.

Beat just until mixed.

Add sugar.

Beat until mixed and smooth.

Add cream cheese.

Beat until mixed and smooth.

Add condensed milk.

Beat until mixed and smooth.

Add lemon juice and zest.

Beat until mixture starts to thicken.

Fold in almond extract.

Beat until thick.

Pour into prepared pie tin.

Chill.

Surprise Angel Food Cake

Ingredients:

1¼ cups confectioner sugar
1 cup flour
12 eggs (1½ cups), whites only, room temperature
1½ teaspoons cream of tartar
1½ teaspoons vanilla extract
½ teaspoon almond extract
¼ teaspoon salt
1 cup sugar

Directions:

Into a mixing bowl, sift confectioner sugar and flour, together, 3 times; set aside.

Using a mixer, high speed, combine egg whites, cream of tartar, vanilla extract, almond extract, and salt.

Gradually add sugar until sugar is dissolved.

Continue beating until stiff peaks form.

Fold in flour mixture, ¼ cup at a time.

Gently spoon into ungreased 10" tube pan.

With knife, slice through batter to remove air pockets.

Bake in reheated 350° oven for 40-45 minutes (or until cake is done)

Invert pan onto cooling rack.

Cool completely before removing cake from pan.

Surprise Cranberry Pie

Ingredients:
2 cups cranberries, fresh
1 cup pecans, chopped
½ + 1 cup sugar
2 eggs
1 cup flour, sifted
⅛ teaspoon of salt
¼ cup butter
½ cup butter, melted

Directions:

In a mixing bowl, combine cranberries, pecans, and ½ cup sugar; set aside.

In a mixing bowl, beat eggs until thick.

Gradually add 1 cup sugar.

Beat well.

Add flour, salt, melted butter, and butter.

Pour over cranberries and nuts.

Mix.

Pour into 9" x 13" glass baking dish.

Bake in preheated 325° oven for 50 minutes.

RECIPE INDEX

Note: Main sections are shown in all-caps/boldfaced type. Subsections are shown in regular upper- and lower-case type:

Almond Crème, 27
American Teen Pâté, 61
Apple-Onion Tea, 105
Apricot Nectar Cake, 209
Apricot Pâté, 62
Arabian Spice, 16
Asparagus and White Grape Pâté, 63
Avocado Soup, 169
Bacon & Broccoli Salad, 185
Bacon-Wrapped Dates, 49
Basic Crepes, 77
Basic Roux, 78
Basic White Cake, 210
Bear Stew, 149
Bearlee Fruit Bread, 781
Bearlee Salad, 186
Beef and Red Wine Stew, 150
Beef Cajun Soup, 170
Beer Venison Casserole , 131
Bite the Beef, 50
(Black) Red Radish Roast Chunky Vegetable Aperitif, 187
Black Rice & Minced Meat Casserole, 133
Bleuet Persil, 171

Blueberry Stuffed Veal Cutlets, 115
Bourbon Orange Glaze Shrimp Babies, 50
BREADS, ROLLS, CREPES, CHIPS, PIE CRUSTS, THICKENERS-DOUGH, 77
Bright Eye Juice, 106
Butter Crust for Pies or Casseroles, 80
Butterfly Butter, 28
Cajun Spice, 16
Cantaloupe Stew, 152
Caramelized Onions, 29
Carrot-Pineapple Spritz, 106
CASSEROLES, 131
Chicken Casserole Topped with Wine Sauce, 134
Chicken Cordon-Bleu Casserole, 135
Chili Butter, 31
Chocolate Hot Pepper Salad, 188
Chocolate Liver Pâté, 64
Chopper Beef, 116
Chunky Artichoke Spread, 52
Ciliegie Fritte, 211
Clarified Butter, 32
Coconut & Corn Stew, 152
Coconut Rum Cheese Pie, 212
Corn Fritters and Spicy Pork Casserole, 137
Crab & Cucumber Puffs, 52
Crab Pâté, 65
Cranberry-Pinot Noir Sauce, 33
"Creamed" PID Stew, 154
Crottin & Coconut on Baguettes, 54
Cucumber Pâté, 66
Curry Spice, 17
DESSERTS, 209
Doux Orange-Potatoe-le Maïs et la Soupe, 172
Dove & Caps Stew, 156
Dragon's Heart Smoothie, 107
English Spice, 18

Fagus Nut Soup, 173
Fatted Lamb Blast Pasta Casserole, 139
Five Cheese Bread Twists, 83
Flavor of Africa Salad, 189
Fruited Plain, 107
Garden Tuna Salad, 190
Gardenia Zucchini, 199
GARNISHES, 27
Golden Rhum Vanille Pudding, 214
Green Chili Stew, 157
Green Tomato Coffee Cake, 215
Hawaiian Spice, 19
Honey Lemon Butter, 34
HORS D'ŒUVRES, 49
Hot Curried Fruit and Bear Meat Casserole, 141
Hot...Red...Neck...Soup, 174
Indian Spice (India), 19
Island Rum Cake, 217
Italian Spice, 20
Killer Compote, 54
Korean Spice, 21
Lamb Patties in Cranberry-Pinot Noir Sauce, 118
Las Espinacas y Alcachofas à la Cazuela, 142
Layered Blueberry Tort, 218
Layered Floating Chocolate Hazelnut Brandy, 220
Lion's Roar, 119
Lobster Cream Stew, 158
MAIN COURSES, 115
Mediterranean Snapper Salad, 191
Mediterranean Spice, 22
Meringue, 34
Mexican Rice, 200
Mexican Spice, 22
Minced Vegetarian Menagerie, 201
Mini Feta Cheese Curls, 84
Mother's Dragon Milk, 109

Mushroom Apple Soup, 175
NATURAL DRINKS, 105
No-Cook Cheese Cake, 221
Nut and Grain Wheat Bread, 86
Nutty Vegetable Stew, 159
Olé de Cerdo Adobado Pan, 87
Olive & Truffle Pâté, 67
Orange Almond Chicken, 121
Orange & Green Iced Tea, 110
Oriental Spice, 23
Ostrich and Tortellini, 123
Over the Rainbow Casserole, 143
Parsley and Lime, 111
PÂTÉS, 61
Pâté à Choux (Puff Pastry), 89
Pea 'n' Pea Pâté, 69
Peach-Tomato Chill, 111
Pear Cream, 35
Peperoni Verdi Gamberoni Farciti, 124
Picante, 35
Pineapple Ham Pâté, 70
Pineapple Picante Beef Casserole, 145
Pineapple Pumpkin Soup, 176
Pinked Butter, 37
Pomegranate Chirp, 112
Poor Man's Saffron Stew, 161
Pork 'n' Pine, 125
Pungent Garlic Dip and Apricots, 55
Raisin Cream, 37
Ravioli-Tortellini Pasta Dough, 90
Red-Pepper Flakes, 24
Red Wine Grape Pâté, 72
Rhubarb Stew, 162
Roasted Asparagus, 202
Rosemary Mozzarella du Pain de Blé, 92
SALADS, 185

Salmon Sting Stew, 163
Salmon Stir, 126
Savory Butter, 38
Savory Lamb Stew, 165
Savory Salt, 24
Savory Toast Points, 93
Sea Bass and White Sauce, 128
SEASONINGS, 15
Shrimp Cream, 38
SIDE DISHES, 199
Simple Butter Croissants, 94
Simple Syrup, 40
Smoky Cheese Ball, 56
Smooth Cream, 40
SOUPS, 169
Sour White Grape Soup, 177
Spiced Ham Boats, 56
Spicy Dried Tomatoes, 41
Spicy Puff Chips, 98
Spinach and Capers Casserole, 146
Spirits of Bread Pudding, 98
Squash Berry Soup, 178
STEWS, 149
Strawberry Minced Meat Salad, 192
Strawberry Pâté, 73
Stuffed Mushrooms with Quail, 57
Sunset Sauce, 43
Sunshine Soup, 179
Surprise Angel Food Cake, 223
Surprise Cranberry Pie, 224
Sweet Butter, 43
The Attorney, 113
Tiger Shrimp & Blackberries on Black Rice, 129
Tiny Ravioli, 59
Tomato & Shrimp Aspic, 194
Tomato Butter, 44

Tomato Oat Bread, 100
Tomato Pecan Green Beans, 203
Tropical Creamed Asparagus Soup, 181
Vanilla Pansy Butternut Squash, 204
Vegetable Pâté, 74
Vegetable Spice, 25
Vegetable Stock, 183
Vegetarian Gratinée, 205
Venison Medallions, 130
Venison Stew, 167
"Weeds" Salad, 195
Whisky Crème, 45
White Butter-Wine, 46
White Carnations, 114
White Sauce, 46
Wild Rice e Trito di Verdure, 206
Wild Rice with Dove Casserole, 147
Wild Violets and Riesling Salad, 196
Wilted Spinach and Broccoli, 207
World Grain Baby Breads, 102
Yellow Beets Red Salad, 197

AUTHORS' BIOS

CECILE CHARLES, an Alpha female, for sure, came from San Francisco to Spokane in the late 1970s as a trained Chef and artist where she took on a Chef de Partie position (Pantry, Saucier, Garde-manager) and was soon established in several kitchens of the city's larger establishments, including the famous Davenport Hotel, delighting the guests with her original recipes, many of which appear in *DINNER WITH CECILE AND WILLIAM*.

Finally, though, her desire to return to painting became too powerful to resist and she opened an arts and antiques boutique, The Heart of Spokane...

http://www.theheartofspokane.com/

...to showcase her artwork and the artwork of other artisans, as well as acquire and sell antiques and collectibles. Not that she ever gave up her passion for fine food and wine, and you can often find her at her favorite Spokane oases for ingredient shopping, as well as wining and dining.

The Davenport Hotel

http://www.thedavenporthotel.com/

Barrister Winery

http://www.barristerwinery.com/

The Vault Restaurant

http://thevaultspokane.com/

Nodland Cellars

http://www.nodlandcellars.com/indexa.htm

Nectar Tasting Room

http://drinknectar.com/

Fushion Flours

http://www.fusionflours.com/Page/contact-us.aspx

Sante' Restaurant

http://www.santespokane.com/www.santespokane.com/Sante.html

Spokane Farmers' Market

http://www.spokanefarmersmarket.org/

Cecile is the author of *COBBLESTONES, THE POCKETBOOK COMPANION, A 24-PARABLE JOURNEY.*

WILLIAM MALTESE is the author (along with Adrienne Z. Milligan) of the best-selling *THE GLUTEN-FREE WAY: MY WAY* (The Traveling Gourmand Series #1), and (along with Bonnie Clark) of the best-selling *BACK OF THE BOAT GOURMET COOKING: AFLOAT, POOL-SIDE, BACKYARD*

(The Traveling Gourmand Series #2), and (along with Bonnie Clark) of the best-selling *EVEN GOURMANDS HAVE TO DIET* (The Traveling Gourmand Series #6), and of the best-selling *WILLIAM MALTESE'S WINE TASTER'S DIARY #1: SPOKANE AND PULLMAN, WASHINGTON* (The Traveling Gourmand Series #3), and (with A.B. Gayle) of the best-selling *WILLIAM MALTESE'S WINE TASTER'S DIARY #2: IN SEARCH OF THE PERFECT PINOT G! AUSTRALIA'S MORNINGTON PENINSULA* (The Traveling Gourmand Series #4); all for the Borgo Press Imprint for Wildside Press. Maltese was born in the Pacific Northwest, has a B.A. in Marketing/Advertising, and spent an honorable tour of duty in the U.S. Army where he achieved the rank of E-5. He began his career writing for men's pulp magazines and has since published more than 200 books...fiction and nonfiction...in every genre...while being honored with a listing in the prestigious *WHO'S WHO IN AMERICA*. For more information on the author, check email and websites:

williammaltese@yahoo.com

http://www.williammaltese.com

http://www.facebook.com/williammaltese

http://www.mxi.myvoffice.com/williammaltese

http://www.myspace.com/williammaltese

http://www.myspace.com/draqual

http://www.myspace.com/flickerwarriors

http://www.myspace.com/maltesecandlegallery

http://www.theglutenfreewaymyway.com

www.ingramcontent.com/pod-product-compliance
Lightning Source LLC
Chambersburg PA
CBHW032108090426
42743CB00007B/279